LUTHER

Other books in the Abingdon Pillars of Theology series

Eugene TeSelle, *Augustine*

Terrence Tice, *Schleiermacher*

Robin W. Lovin, *Reinhold Niebuhr*

Eberhard Busch, *Barth*

ABINGDON PILLARS
OF THEOLOGY

LUTHER

SCOTT H. HENDRIX

Abingdon Press
Nashville

LUTHER

This book is printed on acid-free paper.

Library of Congress Cataloging-in-Publication Data

Hendrix, Scott H.
  Martin Luther / Scott H. Hendrix.
    p. cm. — (Abingdon pillars of theology)
  Includes bibliographical references and index.
  ISBN 978-0-687-65641-7 (pbk. : alk. paper)
  1. Luther, Martin, 1483-1546. I. Title.
  BR332.5.H46 2009
  284.1092—dc22
  [B]

                                                                2008038691

09 10 11 12 13 14 15 16 17 18—10 9 8 7 6 5 4 3 2 1

MANUFACTURED IN THE UNITED STATES OF AMERICA

CONTENTS

PREFACE

This book attempts the nearly impossible: to explain briefly and understandably how and why Martin Luther became a prominent theologian who is still studied and appreciated. No one has read everything he wrote or everything that has been written about him; the sources and interpretations are countless. The "complete" critical edition of his writings, known as the Weimar Edition and started in 1883, the four-hundredth anniversary of Luther's birth, is still not complete. So far it contains more than one hundred volumes. The American Edition of his writings in English has fifty-five volumes, and some of its translations are outdated. Since this book is an introduction for English readers, the American Edition has been quoted and cited, although in some cases a passage has been translated differently or rendered in inclusive language. The bibliography contains mostly sources in English.

Historians and theologians tend to view Luther and the Reformation differently. This book is a blend of perspectives. It has become common for historians to refer to reformations in the plural, but this book deals primarily with the German Reformation and I have stuck with the singular. Some theologians debate whether Luther was Protestant or Catholic, and in some Lutheran circles he is called "evangelical catholic" in order to distinguish Lutherans from Protestants and to emphasize that Luther wanted to reform the old church and not start a new one. Those theological agendas have little to do with the historical Luther. Luther and his German contemporaries called their movement *evangelisch*, and that term included the early Swiss Reformation until the controversy over the Lord's Supper separated the followers of Zwingli (and later Calvin) and the followers of Luther into Reformed and Lutheran churches. Luther used other names for his opponents, most of them not complimentary. Catholics were papists, Zwinglians and Anabaptists were swarming fanatics (*Schwärmer*). Muslims were Turks, because during Luther's lifetime, Islam, in the form of Ottoman armies from Turkey, threatened Christian Europe. Jews were the people of God, but Europe had a long history of Christian anti-Judaism that also infected Luther.

I have retained the word *evangelical* for the early reform movement, even though the word means something different to many English readers. Modern evangelicals associate it not with particular denominations of Christianity, but with characteristics like personal conversion, a literal reading of scripture, specific moral positions, and informal styles of worship. For Luther and other reformers, *evangelical* was applied to a movement or church that was centered on the gospel or good news of Christianity, in contrast to the Roman or papal church that was not, in their view, gospel-centered. Luther's favorite word, however, was not catholic, protestant, or evangelical, but Christian. He saw himself as a reformer of Christendom, not as a reformer of the Roman Catholic Church or the founder of a Protestant church. More about Luther's perspective and reforming agenda is found throughout the book because they were crucial to his theology.

The book covers most of the themes that were prominent in his theology but does not argue that a particular doctrine or topic was *the* key to his thought. Since the book maintains that Luther did not have a single theology, it makes little sense to isolate a theme like justification by faith as the single key to his thought. Nonetheless, the various themes are held together by his reforming agenda and the vision of true Christianity that guided his work. My presentation of these themes is, of course, a result of how I have read and taught Luther's theology (I still use the term) over the years, and in the final chapter I do risk some specific judgments about future interpretations of his thought. Mainly, however, I have tried to let Luther's theology stand on its own, as it must if it is to be a pillar.

Scott H. Hendrix
Professor of Reformation History and Doctrine Emeritus
Princeton Theological Seminary
August 5, 2008

Martin Luther Chronology (1483–1546)

1483	Born November 10 in Eisleben
1505	Master of Arts, Erfurt University; joins the order of Augustinian Hermits
1512	Doctor of Theology, University of Wittenberg
1512–1521	Lectures on Psalms, Romans, Galatians, Hebrews, Psalms
1517	Disputation on scholastic theology; ninety-five theses
1518	Heidelberg disputation; hearing before Cardinal Cajetan
1519	Debate with John Eck in Leipzig; three tracts on the sacraments
1520	*Treatise on Good Works, The Papacy at Rome, Babylonian Captivity of the Church, Address to the Christian Nobility, Freedom of a Christian*
1521	Excommunication; Diet of Worms; declared imperial outlaw
1521–1522	Seclusion at the Wartburg; German New Testament, *Monastic Vows, Postil*
1522	Return to Wittenberg; eight *Invocavit* sermons; *Personal Prayer Book; Estate of Marriage*
1523	Katharina von Bora (1499–1552) flees with other nuns to Wittenberg; *Temporal Authority*
1524	Stops wearing monastic garb; writes against Karlstadt; first Wittenberg hymnal
1525	Commoners revolt; Martin and Katharina marry; *Bondage of the Will*
1526	*German Mass*; birth of son Hans; second edition of *Baptismal Booklet*
1527	Lord's Supper controversy; epidemic in Wittenberg; birth of daughter Elisabeth

1528	*Confession Concerning Christ's Supper*; Saxon visitation; Elisabeth dies; hymn "A Mighty Fortress Is Our God"
1529	Catechisms; Turks besiege Vienna; daughter Magdalena born; evangelical protest at Speyer; Marburg colloquy
1530	Diet of Augsburg; Luther at the Coburg; father Hans dies; *Beautiful Confitemini*
1531	Lectures on Galatians; mother Margaret dies; son Martin born
1532	John Frederick becomes Elector; the Luthers formally receive the Black Cloister (Augustinian monastery) as their dwelling
1533	Son Paul born; academic disputations resumed at Wittenberg
1534	Complete German Bible published; daughter Margarete born
1535	Galatians lectures published; Luther begins to lecture on Genesis
1537	*Smalcald Articles*; Smalcald League meets; suffers kidney ailment
1539	First volume of German writings published; *The Councils and the Churches*
1542	Hymn "Lord Keep Us Steadfast in Your Word"; daughter Magdalena dies
1545	First volume of Latin writings appears; *Against the Papacy, Instituted by the Devil*; finishes Genesis lectures on November 17
1546	Dies February 18 in Eisleben; burial in the castle church at Wittenberg
1547	Wittenberg captured by Emperor Charles V; Katharina and children flee

LAYING THE GROUNDWORK

Martin Luther would be shocked to hear that he is appearing in a series called pillars of theology. To be sure, the professor of biblical interpetation with a doctorate in theology was a theologian. In fact, teaching theology for thirty-four years at the University of Wittenberg brought into Luther's large household, managed by his wife Katharina von Bora, the only salary he ever earned. Still, like most theologians, Luther never thought of himself as *having* a theology. A theologian becomes a pillar of the discipline in the estimation of admiring readers, but they are not the focus of this book.[1] My purpose is to lay the groundwork and identify the pieces that were later used to construct what is now called Luther's theology.

Five principles will help us understand how Luther himself practiced theology.

First, Martin Luther's theology cannot be presented or understood apart from the *world in which he lived*. His life and his work were defined by four contexts: (a) sixteenth-century Germany, where he lived and died; (b) Electoral Saxony, an important territory in the Holy Roman Empire, to which Luther was confined after being declared an outlaw in 1521; (c) the small town and University of Wittenberg, where Luther worked from 1512 to 1546; and (d) the Wittenberg cloister of Augustinian Hermits, in which Luther dwelled initially as a monk and then as a husband and father after his marriage in 1525.

All four settings contributed vital elements to Luther's theological practice. He was reared and schooled in the deep piety of late medieval Germany, and he profited from the intellectual currents of Christian humanism that insisted on the value of education and the study of languages. With the help of his colleagues, he became a gifted translator of the Bible and a master of lucid and expressive German that made him—through the new printing technology—a popular writer. Because the Holy Roman Empire was a patchwork of independent cities and territories, the political clout of the electors of Saxony shielded Luther from the imperial ban and permitted their young university at Wittenberg, founded in 1502, to develop into a haven of the new evangelical theology.

Within the university, Luther was one member of a talented faculty that for the most part supported his judgments of scholastic theology and popular piety. A brilliant young scholar of Greek, Philip Melanchthon, who was hired in 1518 at the age of twenty-one, became his closest theological collaborator, and they formed the core of a Wittenberg movement that Luther described as "our" theology even before Melanchthon arrived on the scene:

> Our theology and St. Augustine are progressing well and with God's help rule at our university. Aristotle is gradually falling from his throne, and his final doom is only a matter of time. It is amazing how the lectures on the *Sentences* are disdained. Indeed, no one can expect to have any students, if [they] do not want to teach this theology, that is, lecture on the Bible or on St. Augustine or another teacher of ecclesiastical eminence.[2]

Courses on the Bible and early Christian thinkers were replacing the lectures on medieval scholastic theology, in which Luther and his colleagues had been trained. Scholasticism was built on principles taken from the Greek philosopher Aristotle, and its basic textbook was the *Sentences*, a collection of debatable opinions from earlier writers that were organized into topics by Peter Lombard (1100–60). In Erfurt, where he was among those monks chosen to pursue an academic career, Luther studied both Aristotle's philosophy and scholastic theology. Like other teachers-to-be he delivered the required lectures on Lombard's *Sentences*, to which he applied the logical skills he had learned from Aristotle and developed during his scholastic training.

Teaching theology on the basis of scripture and Augustine (354–430) departed from the scholastic method, but it was not entirely new. It harkened back to the way theology had been taught in schools attached to cloisters, and it revealed the debt that Luther owed to his monastic heritage. Luther lived as a monk for almost one-third of his life, and the monastic goal of an intentional Christian life, in different dress, made its way into his Reformation theology.

Second, Luther's theology grew out of his *interpretation of scripture*. This axiom is not the same as the principle "by scripture alone" (*sola scriptura*), that is, making scripture the chief authority for theological assertions. As a theologian Luther's job was to glean from the biblical text insights for his students about God and the world. His first attempt, a course on Psalms, lasted two years (1513–15) and made use of explanations by his predecessors. After the psalter Luther lectured on Romans (1515–16), Galatians (1516–17), Hebrews (1517–18), and again on Psalms (1519–21). He had reached only Psalm 22 when he was summoned to Worms in April of 1521, and after he returned to Wittenberg from hiding in 1522, he did not pick up where he had stopped. During the turbulent years that followed, Luther offered his courses on a regular basis. The lectures commonly used for reconstructing his theology are the second series on Galatians, which were delivered in 1531 and published in 1535, and the extensive course on Genesis, on which Luther lectured from 1535 to 1545 and that now take up the first eight volumes of the American Edition.

Although these lectures are sometimes called "commentaries," especially in their edited and printed forms, they were not commentaries in the modern sense of biblical aids but theology in the raw, that is, direct applications of the biblical text to the world of Luther and his students.[3] For that reason Luther's lectures on scripture often sound like sermons and demonstrate how Luther's theology was both biblical and contextual. About two thousand of his actual sermons have been preserved in the Weimar Edition of Luther's works. In 1538 Luther reflected on his early preaching activity: "Often I preached four sermons on one day; during the whole of one Lent I preached two sermons and gave one lecture every day."[4] The sermons are probably the least utilized resource for appreciating Luther's theological mind, although several important treatises developed from sermons or ideas for sermons. For example, the treatise on good works (1520), a major early book, was an exposition of the Ten Commandments, which Luther started as a sermon that outgrew his intention.[5] The catechisms published in 1529 were actually based on sermons. One way or another, therefore, Luther was frequently interpreting scripture when he was thinking, speaking, and writing about theology.

Third, Martin Luther thought of himself as a *teacher* before regarding himself as a theologian or a reformer. In 1520 Luther wrote:

Although I know full well and hear every day that many people think little of me and say that I only write little pamphlets and sermons in German for the uneducated laity, I do not let that stop me. Would to God that in my lifetime I had, to my fullest ability, helped one layperson to be better! I would be quite satisfied, thank God, and quite willing then to let all my little books perish. . . . I will most gladly leave to anybody else the glory of greater things. I will not be ashamed in the slightest to preach to uneducated laypeople and write for them in German.[6]

Luther did not belittle education or academic theology. After all, he was a university professor who debated in Latin with his peers the technical questions of scholastic theology. He prized the doctor of theology degree awarded to him in 1512 and vowed he would not exchange it for all the world's gold. After his excommunication it became the chief warrant for his reforming mission: "God and the whole world bear me testimony that I entered into this work publicly and by virtue of my office as teacher and preacher and have carried it hitherto by the grace and help of God."[7] Although he continued to lecture in Latin until the end of his life, he wrote more books and tracts in German as the reforms made headway. For Luther reform was not yet finished when a new theological curriculum was adopted at the university. Not only clergy-to-be but also working clergy and their parishes needed to be taught a different way of believing, learning, and practicing the faith. That required Luther and his colleagues to preach and write in German and, not to be forgotten, to translate the Bible into the language of the people.

Fourth, Martin Luther was an *occasional theologian*. This phrase does not mean that Luther wrote theology infrequently but that he was prompted to ponder theological topics while facing specific opponents or issues. In other words, he did not spin out of his head long books about God, Christ, or the church, but he had to think about these topics while solving a particular problem or responding to an adversary. In fact, Luther attributed his theological ability to the stiff and persistent opposition he faced: "I myself . . . am deeply indebted to my papists that through the devil's raging they have beaten, oppressed, and distressed me so much. That is to say, they have made a fairly good theologian of me, which I would not have become otherwise."[8]

A good example of this occasional theology is his book on the bound will, written in response to an attack by the prominent Dutch humanist, Erasmus of Rotterdam, who remained loyal to the Roman Church. In his long reply, the title of which is often translated as *The Bondage of the Will*

(1525),[9] Luther defended his conviction that the will was bound to sin until it was liberated by the Holy Spirit. As Luther made his case and tried to refute the biblical evidence brought by Erasmus, he ranged over many topics like the clarity of scripture, the hiddenness of God, the nature of sin, election, freedom of the will, and the grace of Christ. For that reason, *The Bondage of the Will* is often regarded as one of his major theological treatises. Indeed it is, but it does not present those topics in such a complete or systematic way that Luther's comments in other places can be ignored.

Occasionally, Luther would choose the theme of a treatise, as he did in some of his earliest writings for the laity in German: the sacraments, preparation for dying, short expositions of the Ten Commandments, the creed, the Lord's Prayer, the right kind of good works, and Christian freedom. These tracts or pamphlets, especially those published from 1517 to 1520, sold so well that Luther quickly became the most successful religious author of his day. He was aided, of course, by the rapid expansion of the printing industry and the initial scarcity of German material to publish. Still, Luther knew how to present theology so that laity would both understand it and find it useful. In fact, he was more admired for that ability than for the learned Latin volumes (like *Bondage of the Will*) that scholarly adversaries coaxed from his pen.

Fifth, Luther's theology arose from his *reforming agenda*. Although he did, as he wrote, get involved "in the turmoils" with Rome "by accident,"[10] by late 1521 at the latest, while he sat in protective custody at the Wartburg, a purpose for the new evangelical movement that had begun in Wittenberg was crystallizing in Luther's mind. When he returned to the city during the first week of Lent (early March) of 1522, he preached a sermon every day. That series of sermons both undermined the leadership of Andrew Karlstadt, his former colleague, and announced the goal of reform that would echo throughout his writings during the coming years. Changes needed to be made in church rules like fasting, in attitudes toward statues and pictures, and in the way the Lord's Supper was offered and received, but those changes were to be made in the spirit of Christian freedom and the goal of change was to enhance both faith and love in the lives of believers. Luther was upset by the suddenness of Karlstadt's alterations. People felt compelled to accept them before they were ready, and that pressure demonstrated a lack of love and mutual forbearance that Christians should have for one another. Hence, in the spirit of 1 Corinthians 13, Luther preached that possession of the gospel and true faith were of little value if "nobody extends a helping hand to the other, nobody seriously considers the other person, . . . nobody looks after the poor" to see how they might be helped. "This is a pity," he said. "You have heard many sermons about it and all my books are full of it and have one purpose, to urge you to faith and love."[11]

When he said "all my books," Luther was exaggerating, but many of his books and sermons did aim at strengthening the faith and love of believers. As the epitome of his teaching Luther could have cited the tract on Christian freedom that he sent to Pope Leo X. He described it to Leo as a "small book if you regard its size," but he maintained that it contained "the whole of Christian life in a brief form, provided you grasp its meaning."[12] Luther condensed that meaning into two propositions: "A Christian is a perfectly free lord of all, subject to none; a Christian is a perfectly dutiful servant of all, subject to all."[13] Then he explained how the believer becomes free through faith and a dutiful servant of others through love. It was a template of the Christian life that illustrated Luther's way of writing theology—not by constructing an intricate web of theological concepts but by showing readers how they could receive the gifts of faith and love and use them to liberate themselves and to serve others. Luther's desire to change the pattern of Christian living, which he thought had been distorted by medieval clerics, guided the development of his theology and held it together.

CHAPTER TWO

BECOMING LUTHER

The development of Luther's theology was guided not only by his agenda but also by his task as the leader of a new religious movement. He did not become a pillar of theology as Martin Luther the university student, the young monk, or the professor of the Bible; he had to become just Luther, that is, a person so well-known, celebrated, and notorious that he would be recognized by his family name alone. That notoriety found Luther suddenly. It is not quite true that one night he went to bed as Martin Luther, the ordinary monk and professor, and awakened the next morning as Luther, the daring critic of indulgences and challenger of papal supremacy. However, within a few months after the ninety-five theses became public on October 31, 1517, their circulation made his name known in the erudite and clerical circles of Germany and Rome.

The theses were not a manifesto: they were composed in Latin for a university debate, which Luther may have announced by posting them on the door of the castle church. Nevertheless, they did question the value of indulgences, criticize the exaggerated claims made for them, and propose a limit on papal power to grant an indulgence like the one just authorized in collusion with Archbishop Albert of Mainz in order to finance the construction of St. Peter's Basilica in Rome. Luther's decision to send a copy to Albert was fateful. After Albert forwarded the theses to Rome, the curia opened legal proceedings that led to Luther's excommunication in early 1521. By the time he was summoned to appear before Emperor Charles V at Worms in April of the same year, Luther's name was on the lips of many ordinary Germans as well.

After Worms, Luther was kidnapped by his own duke and taken to the Wartburg fortress until Elector Frederick of Saxony could decide what to do about the professor at his cherished university who was now a notorious outlaw in the Holy Roman Empire. That sojourn at the Wartburg from April 1521 to March 1522 concluded the first phase of Luther's career. That phase, usually called the "young Luther," was marked by study at the University of Erfurt, his life as a monk in Erfurt and Wittenberg, his early teaching career, and the initial conflict with the papacy. The writings of this period have been scrutinized for clues to the new theology that led Luther into conflict with Rome, but the timing and content of Luther's "Reformation discovery" are still controversial.

This early period was nonetheless crucial to Luther's development. Once established in the Wittenberg faculty, he initiated a two-front attack on popular piety and on the scholastic theology that supported it. As he pored over scripture and the writings of Augustine, Luther began to have misgivings about the way in which late medieval theologians had interpreted those ancient authorities. The Bible said nothing, as far as Luther could see, about private masses, monastic vows, praying to saints, acquiring indulgences, or other means through which laity were taught to earn salvation. Aristotle's argument that a person became good by doing good works appeared to contradict Paul's declaration that only faith in Christ made one good in God's eyes. Augustine, as Luther read him, became the reformer's guide to Paul's theology and led him to substitute justification by faith for human striving and religious merit as the key to salvation.

Prior to his excommunication the conflict with defenders of papal authority forced Luther to clarify his concept of justification and to develop a view of the church (an ecclesiology) that was broader than Rome had claimed. The title of his treatise, *The Papacy at Rome*, sounds redundant, but it signals Luther's objection to the papal claim that the true church was subject to Rome and to the authority of its bishop. In 1520 Luther had no intention of founding a new church, but he was already convinced that Christianity was a spiritual assembly of believers that extended beyond Rome and could exist in forms other than the Roman Church.

The second phase of Luther's career (1522–30) began with his return to Wittenberg and his rise to leadership of a German evangelical movement. Luther's rejection of Karlstadt's tactics required him and colleagues like Philip Melanchthon to propose their own forms of worship and leadership. Who would ordain priests and appoint them to parishes now that Roman bishops were no longer available? What role should civil officials play in restructuring the churches? What kind of worship would replace the medieval Latin mass and all the private masses that priests and monks had said on behalf of the laity? What should be done with pictures and statues of saints and what would become of former nuns and monks who had renounced their vows and left the cloisters? What should be done with the funds from which clergy had been paid for those private masses and special prayers? By 1522 Luther had expressed his views on most of these matters, but now he had to offer some workable alternatives.

Those proposals came quickly from his pen and contained theological concepts that shaped his thought. For example, the adoption of two kingdoms as an analytical tool arose from Luther's attempt to define the relationship of Christians to civil government; that concept was quickly tested by the social revolution of 1525 known as the Peasants' Revolt. In 1520 Luther had argued that all Christians were priests and that laity were spiritually equal to clergy, but now he and his colleagues had to redefine the office of ministry and the procedures by which ministers were to be chosen and held accountable. In 1523 and 1526 Luther offered versions of the mass as a guide for public worship in evangelical churches. Although they retained much of the liturgy, references to the mass as a sacrifice were removed and the presence of Christ's real body and blood in the sacrament was confirmed. Attacks on the real presence by Karlstadt and Ulrich Zwingli (1524–29) forced Luther to formulate carefully his sacramental and christological views. When priests, monks, and nuns were allowed to marry (including Luther and Katharina von Bora), marriage became a holy estate and not a sacrament. Luther designated the household one of three spheres in which God intended for Christians to live; and he called these spheres true orders, because they replaced the clerical order that had been considered holier than the roles that laypeople occupied.

The Wittenbergers argued vigorously that these proposals had behind them the authority of scripture, which took precedence over regulations and traditions authorized by the church but not supported by the Bible. Their argument presupposed, of course, that they and not their opponents, who also invoked the Bible, were interpreting scripture correctly. During the 1520s, Luther and his colleagues expanded the biblical foundation of their movement. A team of scholars, including Luther, Melanchthon, and the professor of Hebrew, gradually produced a German translation of the Old Testament that complemented Luther's 1522 translation of the New Testament. As he was required to do, Luther lectured on biblical books from both testaments and preached frequently. Some of these lectures and sermons were published, as were occasional pieces that dealt with the Bible. In 1530 he explained and defended his guidelines for translating, and during the Diet of Augsburg, which he was not allowed to attend, he calmed his fears with an exposition of Psalm 118, which he called "the beautiful Confitemini" and his "own beloved psalm."[1]

In 1529 the cities and regions of Germany that had adopted the evangelical movement protested the repeal of their right to make that choice. As a result, Emperor Charles V sought another way to restore religious unity to Germany. He needed money and soldiers from both evangelical (or Protestant) and Catholic rulers in order to stop the Ottoman Turks, who had besieged Vienna in 1529. At the next imperial diet in Augsburg, Charles ordered the Protestants to present an account of their beliefs and a defense of the changes they had made in worship and religious practice. In late June 1530, the Elector John of Saxony and his allies offered the emperor a statement that had been prepared by the Wittenberg theologians and others who agreed with their Lutheran position. This statement, henceforth known as the *Augsburg Confession*, was rejected by Charles on the advice of his Catholic advisors, and Lutheran leaders were ordered to comply with Roman theology and practice.

That order officially launched the confessional confrontation that dominated the third period of Luther's career, which lasted until his death in 1546. By 1530 Luther had been notorious for over a decade, and the evangelical segment that hewed to his theology of the sacraments was slowly being labeled Lutheran. While negotiations between Lutherans and their opponents continued, Luther fulfilled his duties at the university by giving significant courses on Galatians and Genesis, responding with his colleagues to requests for political advice from the new Elector John Frederick (1532–47), and defending the Lutheran movement against adversaries. His polemic became harsher during this period. The precarious situation of Protestants, given respite but still legally in defiance of the emperor, played a role in Luther's blunt, sometimes crass and insulting, language. He regarded the gospel (his name for the core of the Lutheran message) as beset on all sides by enemies—by the Roman church, by radical dissenters like Anabaptists, by Protestants in the Reformed movement started by Ulrich Zwingli, even by Jews and Muslims. Their opposition was a sign of the last days during which God's archenemy, the devil, was launching an all-out attack on the gospel.

During this period, therefore, Luther's theology was formulated in a context that was more threatening to him than earlier stages of the

Reformation. He redoubled his efforts to convince students and laity that "our theology" was true and reminded them not infrequently how oppressive life "under the papacy" had been. In the lectures on Galatians (1531) he expounded justification in such detail that these lectures have become a primary textbook of his thought. In the lectures on Genesis, which lasted for ten years, he developed a theology of history that extended the promises of God, given to the patriarchs and matriarchs, into his own times. After centuries of being suppressed, so Luther taught, those promises had been recovered and renewed in the Reformation. They now offered hope and comfort to him and to all who believed that God would faithfully fulfill his promises and preserve the true church forever.

When Luther died, the fate of the German Reformation was still undecided. Indeed, the future looked bleaker than ever. In 1545 the Council of Trent began to debate and codify the objections of the Roman church to the Protestant movement and to decide for itself what reforms were necessary. The political strength of the stalwart Protestant leader, Philip of Hesse, had been neutralized by Emperor Charles V, who finally lost patience with his Lutheran subjects. In 1547 his army defeated their forces and captured Wittenberg. By cooperating with the new Lutheran elector of Saxony, who was awarded the title after agreeing to fight on the emperor's side, Melanchthon and his followers were able to avert the closing of the university and keep alive the hope of reform. Other Lutheran theologians, however, scorned that cooperation and established strongholds first in Magdeburg and later at the University of Jena. Both sides claimed to be the true heirs of Luther and his theology, but Melanchthon's opponents won the war of labels. They became known as the gnesio- (genuine) Lutherans, and Melanchthon's followers became the Philippists. The conflicts over Luther's theology among his followers had begun in the 1520s, and they continued even after 1555 when Lutheran churches in Germany were legally tolerated. The process of becoming a public figure started and matured in controversy, and Luther, even as a pillar of theology, has remained controversial ever since.

CHAPTER THREE

SHAPING A THEOLOGIAN

The three phases of Luther's life, so different from one another, prevented his theology from ripening early into a finished product. It developed gradually in the course of his teaching and in response to the opposition he faced. In 1532 he declared: "I have not learned my theology all at once; rather the attacks on me have forced me to keep digging more deeply."[1] Much of that digging was done in the Bible, but it was not the only influence on his theology. His thought was eclectic. It received impulses from a variety of sources, the most important of which were monasticism, scholasticism, the writings of Augustine, mysticism, and humanism.

Monasticism

Twenty years elapsed between Luther's entry into the monastery and his marriage, the event that publicly broke his vow of celibacy and removed the ambiguity around his rejection of the monastic life. Luther continued to wear monastic garb three years after he had written against the traditional claims for monastic vows. Most of his fellow monks had left the black cloister, as the house of the Augustinians was called, but Luther was still living there in 1525 when he and Katharina von Bora were married. Just prior to the wedding, Luther's prince and protector, Elector Frederick, died, but his brother, the new Elector John, was a steadfast supporter of the Reformation and permitted the Luthers to make the monastery their home. Altogether, as a monk and a married man, Martin lived forty-one of his sixty-two years in cloistral surroundings.

On balance, Luther's life as a monk was a frustrating experience, but those years also shaped positively both his piety and his theology. In the first place, monasticism taught Luther to take the Christian life with utmost seriousness. Monks and nuns were (and still are) called religious because they made Christianity their full-time profession and strove after a perfect Christian life. Although Luther rejected the manner in which monks and nuns claimed perfection because they had withdrawn from the world, he appreciated in principle their dedication to a Christian way of living. In place of monasticism he constructed a new pattern of Christian dedication that was available to all believers, not just to those who left the world for the cloister. *The Freedom of A Christian* (1520) is the most explicit presentation of that pattern, and faith and love, the twin foci of his reforming agenda, appear over and over in his descriptions of the Christian life.[2]

Owing to its emphasis on Christian living, monasticism was first and foremost concerned with the practice of Christianity, and so was Luther's reform. His proposal to reconstruct the Christian life around faith and love required serious theological effort as well, but his experience as a monk kept Luther's theology eminently practical. For that reason, his theology does not lend itself to a comprehensive, systematic presentation. Even though he was acquainted with scholastic theology, it did not serve the life of faith that being a monk had taught him to put first.

Scripture

Luther's years as an Augustinian friar immersed him in scripture and in the devotional writings of late medieval Christianity. He once claimed that he had never seen a Bible until he was twenty years old, but life in the monastery quickly filled that hole. He obtained a copy and read it avidly: "I began to read the Bible, reread it, and read it again."[3] With the other monks at daily worship he sang through the entire Psalter every week, and at meals excerpts from scripture and the church fathers were read aloud. No wonder, then, that Luther knew the Psalter almost by heart and that his writings were saturated with biblical references and allusions. They were not, however, always accurately cited or quoted as modern scholars would do, probably because he seldom had to look up the passage he wanted to use.

Moreover, Luther's job was to lecture on the Bible. He not only studied the text but he also consulted late medieval commentaries with their interpretations. One commentary consisted of marginal notes or glosses printed on each page around the biblical text to which they referred. These glosses, compiled for centuries from early Christian writers like Augustine, were by Luther's time fixed in print and gave him additional access to those theologians and their views. The commentaries and the biblical text itself were in Latin and known only to scholars, monks, and preachers who had access to the books and could read them. Most laypeople did not have a Bible to read, although eighteen German editions, illustrated with woodcuts, appeared prior to Luther's German New Testament in 1522.[4] Luther, however, studied the Bible with regularity and intensity long before he had to debate its authority, and he owed this deep knowledge to his monastic heritage.

Scholasticism

The term refers to the way theology was taught and written in medieval universities. In 1519, after praising lovers of scripture and condemning various schools of thought, Luther wrote: "I know what scholastic theology did for me and how much I owe it. I am glad that I escaped from it, and for this I thank Christ my Lord. They do not have to teach it to me for I already know it! Nor do they have to bring it any closer to me, for I do not want it."[5] Luther often criticized scholasticism as if it were a uniform method, but he could also identify different schools that used the method, for example, "Scotists, Thomists, Albertists, modernists, and all the sects into which these are subdivided."[6] His teachers at Erfurt had initiated Luther into the "modernist" school, so named because it developed after Thomas Aquinas and the scholastics of the thirteenth century (the "old" way). Modernists were also called "nominalists" or "Ockhamists" after the English Franciscan theologian, William of Ockham (d. ca. 1350), its best-known architect. Luther called himself an Ockhamist, once apparently with tongue in cheek, but he read more of the nominalist theologian Gabriel Biel (d. 1495), who was still alive during Luther's childhood. Biel wrote a long analysis of the canon of the mass (the eucharistic prayer), and his lectures on Lombard's *Sentences* were also known to Luther. Through Biel's works he acquired a secondhand knowledge of Thomas and other scholastic authors.

As indicated by his words, the influence of scholastic theology on Luther was both negative and positive. For example, he made fun of the scholastic method but he found useful one of its tools: making distinctions within concepts in order to solve theological problems. Nominalism also had a specific influence. Its view of grace and how grace brought justification and salvation was rejected by Luther. Its concept of divine power, however, appealed to the reformer. Nominalists distinguished God's absolute power from God's ordered power. God's absolute power enabled them to say that in principle God could save humanity however God pleased, but the ordered power enabled them to say that God decided to save humanity in a specific way—through the church and sacraments—and promised not to change the divine mind. God's ordered power was expressed through words, promises, and covenants, which were revealed in scripture and were absolutely reliable. That power made scripture and trust in God's Word more reliable than human reason, and Luther would capitalize on that reliability.

Augustine

Writings by the bishop of Hippo in North Africa had so great an impact on the Middle Ages that almost every theologian could claim to be Augustinian. Luther, however, had good reason to believe that he was following Augustine more faithfully than his predecessors had done. He belonged to the monastic order named for Augustine, and his mentor and superior in the order, John Staupitz (d. 1524), was influenced by Augustine's teaching on grace and predestination. In 1506, the collected works of Augustine were published and Luther began to read them soon thereafter. He later reported that he gained respect for Augustine and devoured his writings because of what he said, not because he was the patron of Luther's order. Indeed, Luther referred to Augustine well over a thousand times, mostly without a specific reference. Augustine's writings, especially his treatise on the spirit and the letter, were especially important for Luther's early lectures on Psalms, Romans, Galatians, and Hebrews. Luther was reading Augustine more for understanding the Bible than for Augustine himself, and in 1518 he named Augustine the most trustworthy interpreter of Paul.

Two features of Augustine's thought had the greatest influence on Luther. First, the primacy of grace. It was crucial to Luther's campaign against the new Pelagians (his term) as it had been for Augustine against the Pelagians of the fourth and fifth centuries. The new Pelagians were the nominalist theologians whom Luther accused of teaching that believers could earn justification by exercising their natural powers without the aid of grace. Statements rejecting that teaching were debated at Wittenberg in early September 1517, almost two months before the ninety-five theses on indulgences. Luther also agreed with Augustine that God's election or predestination of believers backed up the primacy of divine grace, although he did not stress predestination to the extent Augustine had done.

Second, the neo-Platonic philosophy of Augustine left its mark on Luther. He was never a dualist, as Augustine once had been, but Luther distinguished sharply between good and evil, believing fervently in the reality of both God and the devil. God remained sovereign, but sin, death, and the devil were real enemies of that sovereignty and held humanity in their thrall. Nevertheless, those enemies were not equal to or independent of God, and the story of salvation was the story of how God in Christ defeated them and continued to bring them into submission. For both Augustine and Luther sin was fundamentally idolatry, not the worship of evil but the worship of inferior divine gifts as if they were gods. Moreover, to be liberated from sin was to live already in the kingdom of Christ, a new realm of existence not unlike Augustine's city of God in its pilgrim journey through this world.

Mysticism

Was Martin Luther also a mystic? This question is constantly debated because the answer varies according to the definition of mysticism employed as a standard. If it is defined as the inward experience of God, then most scholars agree that Luther's theology had a significant mystical component. If it is defined as union with God, then scholars are more skeptical.

Luther was familiar with the writings of some mystics and made numerous comments about them. He referred appreciatively to the Cistercian abbot, Bernard of Clairvaux (d. 1153), while he rejected the negative mysticism of Pseudo-Dionysius, a sixth-century writer whose ideas were embraced by most medieval theologians. Of special importance was the German mystical preacher John Tauler (d. 1361), whose sermons he studied with colleagues under the aegis of Staupitz.[7] In them he claimed to have found "more solid and sincere theology than is found in all the scholastic teachers of all the universities."[8] Luther also wrote

16

a preface for the mystical treatise known as *A German Theology*, published at his initiative in 1518. He learned more from it, he said, than from any books except the Bible and St. Augustine "about God, Christ, humanity, and all things."[9]

Mysticism was a program for union with God that claimed to be more practical and experiential than scholastic theology, and the same can be said of Luther's theology if that union is brought about through Christ and not human striving. Luther frequently expressed the wonder of justification with the same image that medieval mystics had used: a trade between Christ and the soul called the "marvelous exchange." Luther also used the image very early in a letter of encouragement to an Augustinian brother who had recently been transferred out of Wittenberg:

> Now I should like to know whether your soul, tired of its own righteousness, is learning to be revived by the righteousness of Christ and to trust in him. . . . My dear friar, learn Christ and him crucified. Learn to praise him and, despairing of yourself, say: "Lord Jesus, you are my righteousness, just as I am your sin. You have taken upon yourself what is mine and have given to me what is yours. You have taken upon yourself what you were not and have given me what I was not." Beware of aspiring to such purity that you will not wish to be looked upon as a sinner, or to be one. For Christ dwells only in sinners. . . . Learn from him that, just as he has received you, so he has made your sins his own and has made his righteousness yours.[10]

There is more to be said about the experiential component of Luther's theology, but his adoption of the marvelous exchange is testimony to the impact that Christ-centered mysticism had on his thought.

Humanism

In sixteenth-century Germany this scholarly movement was gradually taking over schools like the University of Wittenberg. Its core was the study of ancient languages and classical thought, and its delivery system was educational reform. Christian humanists devoted their energy to the biblical text and to the works of early Christian writers like Origen, Augustine, and Jerome. Critical editions of their works by prominent scholars such as Erasmus of Rotterdam were appearing in print while Luther studied in Erfurt and began teaching in Wittenberg. The curriculum revision in Wittenberg took advantage of those publications and added new professors of Hebrew and Greek, like Philip Melanchthon, to its faculty. In 1516 Erasmus published his critical edition of the Greek New Testament, and Bible study was never again the same.

Unlike many reformers, Luther was not trained specifically in a humanist atmosphere, but his knowledge of classical literature was broad and in Wittenberg he pushed the humanist agenda. He supported the curricular reform in his department and raved about Melanchthon and the importance of teaching languages. By himself at the Wartburg he embarked on a translation of the New Testament into German and, with colleagues, labored over a translation of the Old Testament until a complete German Bible could be published at Wittenberg in 1534. Despite his argument with Erasmus over the power of the human will (sometimes cast as a debate between a humanist and a monk), Luther advocated new and better public schools, as well as more intensive study of languages and the classics, and he admonished parents to keep their children in school. Humanism was the force behind educating a new generation of evangelical pastors and laypeople, and without it the Reformation would have looked quite different.

Chapter Four

Two Realizations

Many attempts to find the origin of Luther's theology start with the account of his "Reformation discovery" in the preface to the first volume of his collected Latin writings, which appeared in 1545. In fact, there was not one but there were two Reformation discoveries or two accounts of Luther's distinctive contributions to the reforming program called the Reformation. The first account describes a crucial theological insight, but it also illustrates Luther's use of the Bible and reveals the impact of his early monastic life. The second account describes a vital personal calling, but it also contains clues to Luther's theological development and to his monastic experience. The accounts complement each other, and it is necessary to consider both in order to gain a balanced picture of the monk and professor of Bible who became a reformer and theologian.

The first account, which scholars have labeled his "discovery," appears at the end of the 1545 preface and is a flashback to early 1519 when Luther began his second lecture course on Psalms:

> Meanwhile, I had already during that year returned to interpret the Psalter anew. I had confidence in the fact that I was more skillful after I had lectured in the university on St. Paul's epistles to the Romans, the Galatians, and the Hebrews. Indeed I had been captivated with an extraordinary ardor for understanding Paul in the epistle to the Romans. But until then it was not cold blood around the heart but a single word in chapter 1 [:17], "In it the righteousness of God . . . ," which, according to the custom and use of all the teachers, I had been taught to understand philosophically regarding the formal or active righteousness (as they call it) with which God is righteous and punishes the unrighteous sinner.[1]

Luther had been preparing lectures on the Bible since 1513, but when he came to Paul's words in Romans 1:16-17 he was stumped. Verse 17 said that the righteousness or justice of God was revealed in "it," that is, in the gospel, which in verse 16 Paul had called a divine power that brought salvation to all who believed. Since that power was good news, Luther could not understand how the righteousness of God, revealed in the same gospel, could be bad news, that is, a standard against which God measured and judged sinners. Luther could have stopped at that point and announced his resolution of the dilemma, but instead he switched to a description of his experience as a monk:

> Although I lived as a monk without reproach, I felt that I was a sinner before God with an extremely disturbed conscience. I could not believe that [his anger] was placated by my satisfaction. I did not love, no, I hated the righteous God who punished sinners, and secretly if not blasphemously, certainly murmuring greatly, I was angry with God and said: "As if, indeed, it is not enough that miserable sinners, eternally lost through original sin, are crushed by every kind of calamity by the Ten Commandments without having God add pain to pain by the gospel and also threatening us by the gospel with his justice and wrath!" Thus I raged with a fierce and troubled conscience. Nevertheless I nagged Paul about that passage, most ardently desiring to know what St. Paul intended.[2]

Luther was stumped by Romans 1:17, not only for theological reasons, but also for personal reasons. He was trying to be a perfect monk, but no matter how strictly he obeyed the rule or how scrupulously he confessed, he still felt that he was an unworthy sinner who could not live up to the standard of God's justice. Being unable to keep the Ten Commandments was bad enough because it only increased the burden of original sin, but to be threatened by the gospel was intolerable. He became so frustrated that he pounded on the biblical text looking for an answer. The problem was not only a philosophical disagreement with scholastic theology; it was also a religious crisis that he attempted to solve by intensive biblical study. That study took him beyond the book of Romans and finally paid off:

> At last, by the mercy of God, meditating day and night, I gave heed to the context of the words: "In it the righteousness of God is revealed, as it is written, 'They who through faith are righteous will live.'" I began to understand that the righteousness of God meant that those who were righteous lived by a gift of God, which is the passive righteousness by which God justifies us through faith, as it is written: "They who through

faith are righteous shall live" [Habakkuk 2:4]. I felt I was altogether born again and had entered paradise through open gates. A completely different face of the entire scripture showed itself to me and I ran through the scriptures from memory. I found in other terms an analogy: the work of God, that is, what God does in us; the power of God, with which God makes us strong; the wisdom of God, with which God makes us wise; likewise the strength of God, the salvation of God, the glory of God.[3]

Luther's experience of relief and liberation was so memorable that it seems as if he made the discovery suddenly. His own words, however, belie that impression. He realized that God's justice was good news only after painstaking study showed that it was granted through faith and not earned through meritorious deeds. Luther would have called it a realization instead of discovery because for him it had always been present in scripture. That realization came gradually between 1513 and 1519. He did not immediately leave the monastery, but he did question religious practices that failed to bring the same liberation, joy, and security that he now experienced: monasticism, endowed masses and prayers, the penitential system with its indulgences, invoking the saints for help, pilgrimages to their shrines, and compulsory almsgiving and fasting. Discovering justification by faith affected his theology and his experience, his thought and his life. His condemnation by pope and emperor forced him to reconsider what kind of Christian he was.

The monk Martin became Luther, as we saw earlier, through the acclaim he enjoyed as a leader of the evangelical movement. Inwardly, however, he had to identify the nature of that role and become convinced that he belonged in it. The account of this realization is the subject of a letter that Luther addressed to his father Hans in 1521. Like the book that it dedicates, Luther's *Judgment on Monastic Vows*, the letter was written in Latin while he was in exile at the Wartburg castle, and, if it was mailed as well as printed, it had to be translated into German for his father to read. Presumably, then, the letter was more public than private. It was Luther's proclamation that he had left behind his old role as a monk and assumed a new role that today is called a reformer.

One purpose of a dedication is to show appreciation, and accordingly Luther thanked his father, who was disappointed that his son chose the monastic life, for trying to dissuade him. Luther recalls the tense encounter between the two men at the Augustinian cloister in Erfurt when his father attended the first mass celebrated by the young monk and priest. Luther maintained that his vow had been prompted by a terrifying thunderstorm, but his father retorted that he hoped his son had not suffered a delusion. Hans's disapproval cut Luther to the quick, and the psychiatrist Erik Erikson named their strained relationship as one reason why Luther suffered from a pathology that "at times approached . . . a borderline psychotic state."[4] In reality, however, the rift between father and son was healed, and the role reversal that Luther described in this letter was part of the healing.

Instead of blaming his father, who in 1521 was still very much alive, Luther blamed himself for not obeying his father, as the Fourth Commandment required, and gave Hans credit for trying to shield him from a way of life that his father considered dangerous and ill-suited to a young man of promise. Luther realized that his father's disapproval was an expression of fear for his son's future[5] and, moreover, that his father's fear was a measure of how much Hans cared about his son.[6] Luther admitted that his father had been right, but he also discovered a divine purpose in his own refusal to obey. What his father did not do—namely, rescue him from the monastery—God himself had done and was now bestowing upon him a divine calling. Luther described the conversion in this way:

> Shall I belong to the cowl or shall not rather the cowl belong to me? My conscience has been freed and that is the most complete liberation. Therefore I am still a monk and not a monk. I am a new creature, not of the pope but of Christ. . . . Who can doubt that I am in the ministry of the word? And it is plain that the authority of parents must yield to this service, for Christ says: "He who loves father or mother more than me is not worthy of me" [Matthew 10:37].[7]

It was no accident that the liberation claimed for himself was the same freedom about which he wrote one year earlier in *Freedom of a Christian*. In that book the freedom of faith inevitably led to serving the neighbor, and Luther realized that his own freedom from the papacy and the monastery now brought with it a new service both to Christ and to others. He called this service a "ministry of the word," and by it he meant bringing the same liberation to others or, as he put it, making them children of Christ, their only master. Recalling for his father the divine operation in the history of their relationship, Luther wrote:

> I am sending [you] this book, in which you may see by what signs and wonders Christ has absolved me from the monastic vow and granted me such great liberty. Although he has made me the servant of all, I am,

nevertheless, subject to no one except to him alone. He is himself (as they say) my immediate bishop, abbot, prior, lord, father, and teacher; I know no other. Thus I hope Christ has taken from you one son in order that he may begin to help the sons of many others through me.[8]

Without this role reversal, Luther's theology would not have developed as it did. With it, however, Luther's ministry of the word became a missionary movement under his direction. The agenda was to Christianize Germany with an uncorrupted gospel, and the apostolic mission recounted in Acts became a paradigm for Luther and his colleagues. Addressing Melanchthon several months before the letter to his father, Luther compared Wittenberg to Antioch and urged his colleagues at the university to go forth like early Christian missionaries: "You lecture, Amsdorf lectures; Jonas[9] will lecture; do you want the kingdom of God to be proclaimed only in your town? Do not others also need the gospel? Will your Antioch not release a Silas or a Paul or a Barnabas for some other work of the Spirit?"[10] Luther claimed not to mind if the Lord "opened a door for the word" in bigger towns because the harvest was large and little Wittenberg had more preachers than it needed.[11]

Luther's new role had four important consequences for his theology. First, his sermons and his writings continually challenged readers to become genuinely Christian in a way that was similar to his own experience. He described freedom of faith and the service of love not as doctrines to be learned but as a way of living to be embraced; and he was able to write about them so engagingly and describe the theological implications so sharply because it had happened to him—a human being and a trained theologian. More than once Luther used his own experience as an argument for the correctness of a theological position.

Second, the conviction of being accountable to Christ alone reinforced the Christocentric dimension of Luther's theology. The opposite of idolatry was not just faith, but faith in Christ, who was the exclusive path to freedom and a guilt-free conscience. Christianizing Germany meant something different, therefore, from making people more committed to the faith they already knew. It meant changing Christianity in order to make Christ central to its faith and especially to its piety. Strengthening faith in Christ became the criterion for judging whether or not a specific practice could be kept or had to be discarded. Luther himself was leaving the old authorities behind and adopting Christ as his only master. He wanted to bring the rest of Germany into the same liberating subjection that he had experienced.

Third, a sense of urgency infused his writings. The eschatological awareness that had already framed his conflict with the papacy was transferred to the evangelical movement. The last days were at hand, and the mission of spreading the good news had only a small window of opportunity:

> For you know that God's word and grace is like a passing shower of rain which does not return where it has already been. It has been with the Jews, but when it's gone it's gone, and now they have nothing. Paul brought it to the Greeks; but again when it's gone it's gone, and now they have the Turk; Rome and the Latins also had it; but when it's gone it's gone, and now they have the pope. You Germans need not think that you will have it forever, for ingratitude and contempt will not make it stay. Therefore, seize it and hold it fast, whoever can; for lazy hands are bound to have a lean year.[12]

This eschatological urgency went hand in hand, as it does in scripture, with frequent references to the kingdom of God and a faithful remnant. Preaching on the Good Shepherd in 1523, Luther said, paraphrasing Paul:

> Now there is one church or congregation, one faith, one hope, one love, one baptism. . . . That is still true today and will remain true until the last day. It does not necessarily mean that the entire world and everyone in it will believe in Christ, for we must always have the holy cross with us, that is, a majority who persecute Christians. We must, therefore, always preach the gospel in order to convert at least a few; for the kingdom of Christ is never finished but always in process.[13]

Finally, Luther began to identify with the apostle Paul and to act as if the evangelical movement belonged to him. Consequently, his theology kept the sharp polemical edge it had assumed during the conflict over indulgences, and it became increasingly inflexible. He refused to negotiate points of disagreement like the presence of Christ in the Lord's Supper. When he debated this topic with the Swiss reformers at Marburg in 1529, he insisted that he was right and accused Zwingli of having a different spirit.[14] The more opposition he faced, the more he restricted true Christianity to his followers alone. His disdain extended to other believers and unbelievers alike. All were treated as enemies of the gospel: Turks, Jews, papists, and sacramentarians, the last category including Protestants and dissenters who rejected infant baptism and the real presence. Luther regarded them as agents of the devil who, in the last days of the world, had unleashed a final assault upon Christendom.

Luther's harshness and inflexibility have been attributed to his physical maladies, but a more crucial factor was the conviction that he was accountable to no one other than Christ. Instead of giving him confidence in the face of opposition, this exclusive accountability led him to dismiss the views of his opponents. In 1521, for example, he accused a former sympathizer turned radical critic, Thomas Müntzer, of enjoying and using "the fruits of our victory" when he had "done no battle for it and risked no bloodshed to attain it."[15] Luther's realization that he was free by faith was sometimes exaggerated to the point of neglecting love for the neighbor. Believing in Christ alone and being subject to Christ alone were not easy to reconcile or to put into practice. Luther was not the only reformer to make that discovery.

CHAPTER FIVE

LIVING WITH THE BIBLE

The phrase *sola scriptura* (scripture alone) is often associated with Martin Luther's appeals to the authority of scripture, but Luther's relationship with the Bible was much deeper and richer than the phrase suggests. Throughout his career, Luther was involved with scripture on a daily basis: as a monk he heard it and chanted it every day; as a professor of biblical interpretation he studied it and lectured on it almost every semester. He preached mostly on biblical texts, and was regularly occupied with translating biblical books into German. Luther lived, as it were, in the biblical world and viewed his own world through that lens, but he was no twentieth-century fundamentalist. He endorsed critical study of the Bible that was being introduced and promoted by the humanist movement, and he benefited from its fruits.

The Text

After he arrived at the Wartburg in May of 1521, Luther reported that he was sitting "all day, drunk with leisure," and "reading the Bible in Greek and Hebrew."[1] In December he wrote to his Augustinian colleague in Erfurt, John Lang:

> I shall be hiding here until Easter. In the meantime, I will finish the postil and translate the New Testament into German, an undertaking our friends request. I hear you are also working on this. Continue as you have begun. I wish every town had its own interpreter, and that this book

alone, in all languages, would live in the hands, eyes, ears, and hearts of all people.[2]

Luther completed the translation in less than three months. Known as his September testament because it was published in that month of 1522, the first printing of three thousand to five thousand copies sold out in three months. It was reprinted in December, and between 1522 and 1534 eighty-seven editions of his New Testament appeared in high German, an early Saxon version of modern German, and nineteen editions appeared in low German, the dialect spoken in parts of north Germany. The total number of copies distributed for sale may have reached two hundred thousand.

The speed and popularity of Luther's translation are remarkable, but his letter to Lang reveals that it was no solitary undertaking. Luther and his colleagues were in it together. The "friends" who requested it included Philip Melanchthon, whom Luther saw during a secret visit to Wittenberg earlier in December. As Luther had heard, John Lang was producing a German translation of the Gospel of Matthew, and Luther's last sentence, a paraphrase of Erasmus's introduction to his critical Greek version, indicated that Luther welcomed other translations and saw his own as one among many. At the Wartburg Luther had in hand Greek New Testaments prepared by Erasmus and by another humanist, Nicholas Gerbel, who lived in Strasbourg. After listing for Gerbel the writings he had completed during the first five months at the Wartburg, Luther noted how many were in German and said: "I am born for my Germans, whom I want to serve."[3] The humanist movement inspired in Luther and others not only the critical study of the biblical text but also a concerted effort to make accessible to the laity a text they could read.

One work already in print, wrote Luther, was "my German exposition of the epistles and gospels for each Sunday of the church year."[4] It was the "postil" that Luther also mentioned to Lang. Derived from the Latin *post illa verba* ("after those words"), the term *postil* referred to comments on a biblical text that appeared after the text itself. Luther's postil was a running exposition of the lectionary, the appointed readings for Sundays and festival days in the church year. Before he left Wittenberg for Worms, he had started a Latin postil for Advent, the first season of the church year, but at the Wartburg he decided to start over and completed a postil in German for both Advent and Christmas. Eventually, five separate postils were published in various editions, and they became one of the most widely read and influential Luther texts.

During the 1520s Luther was part of a team led by the professor of Hebrew, Matthew Aurogallus, that prepared a German translation of the Old Testament. As they worked on the book of Job, Luther remarked that three of them could scarcely translate three lines every four days. Accordingly, the German Old Testament appeared slowly, in sections, until they were consolidated with the New into a complete German Bible published at Wittenberg in 1534. The volume contained numerous woodcut illustrations that were prepared, with Luther's consultation, in the workshop of Hans Lufft, who printed many of his works. Luther continued to make changes in the translation, and revised versions appeared before and after his death in 1546.

Teaching

Luther's lectures and other writings on the Bible made up the chief part of his academic work. It was a labor of love.[5] For the most part he lectured only once on a biblical book, but he did give two courses each on Psalms and on Galatians. In 1519 his second set of lectures on the first five psalms was published and dedicated to Elector Frederick of Saxony. Luther called this second exposition "vastly different" from the first and declared: "There is no book in the Bible to which I have devoted as much labor as to the Psalter."[6] Moreover, he denied that he had grasped the correct meaning of the psalms "in every particular." It was enough, he said, "to have understood some of the psalms, and those only in part. The Holy Spirit reserves much for himself, so that we may always remain his pupils."[7] A biblical text did not have a single fixed meaning that was valid for all time. Luther claimed he saw some things in the text that Augustine did not see and he knew that others would find meanings that he had not seen. Some interpreters came "closer to the Spirit" than others, but lesser lights should not be despised.

Luther interpreted the psalms not only in the classroom but also for people undergoing hardships. When the Lutheran pastor and his congregation in Miltenberg were forced by the archbishop of Mainz to revert to the Roman Church, Luther sent them a present of Psalm 120 in German with a brief commentary, so that "you may see how God comforts you through his scriptures and how you should pray for protection against the lying slanderers and raving persecutors."[8] As he anxiously awaited the outcome of the Diet of Augsburg in 1530, he consoled himself by reading and writing about Psalm 118. Of verse 17, "I shall not die, but I shall live, and recount the deeds of the LORD," which became his motto, he wrote:

> This verse is a masterpiece for the way in which the psalmist removes death from our sight and refuses to acknowledge dying and sin. Instead, he admits nothing but life, so indelible are the images he presents, for whoever does not see death lives forever, as Christ says: "Very truly, I tell you, those who keep my word will never see death" (John 8:51). They immerse themselves so deeply in life that death is swallowed up and vanishes because with solid faith they hang onto the right hand of God. In this sense have all the saints sung this verse and will keep singing it forever.[9]

Luther's first course on Galatians (1516–17) was reconstructed on the basis of student notes discovered in the early twentieth century, but a heavily revised version had already been published in 1519 and 1523. He sent two copies of the 1519 edition to his Augustinian mentor and superior Staupitz with the revealing comment:

> Reverend Father, I am sending you two copies of my foolish Galatians. They do not please me as much as they did at first, and I see they could have been explained more clearly and completely. But who can do everything at once? Moreover, who can be productive all the time? Nevertheless, I am confident that this Paul is clearer than others have made him before, even if it does not yet satisfy my stomach.[10]

Luther returned to the task in 1531 when he delivered between five and eleven lectures on each chapter of the book. These lectures were transcribed and expanded into print-ready form from extensive notes that had to be collated and edited. Hence they did not appear until 1535, and a revised version was issued already in 1538. By that time, in the classroom Luther's longest course, the ten-year lectures on Genesis, was already underway.

Interpretation

When he lectured on Galatians the second time, Luther had a specific theological agenda: "Paul wants to establish the doctrine of faith, grace, the forgiveness of sins or Christian righteousness, so that we may have a perfect knowledge and know the difference between Christian righteousness and all other kinds of righteousness."[11] Most of the time, however, the agenda was not that focused. His hermeneutical principles were flexible, a blend of goals that modern study of the Bible keeps apart by drawing a sharp line between understanding a text and contemplating it devotionally.

Like most of his predecessors Luther treated the Bible as a unity. The Old and New Testaments belonged together and were a book for Christians. Christ was already present in the scripture of the Hebrews because the trinitarian God was active at creation and thereafter by electing Israel to be God's servant to the nations. For Luther Israel lived under divine promises—God's word to the serpent in Genesis 3:15, promises made to the patriarchs, and prophecies of the Messiah. Israel lived under those promises without seeing their fulfillment in Jesus of Nazareth, but Luther saw therein an important analogy to the Christian life. Although Christians believed the divine promises were fulfilled in the life, death, and resurrection of Jesus, they still lived with a promise of future things, the promise of Christ's return to complete God's redeeming work. Christians were not unlike the faithful of the Old Testament and could learn much from their faith and example.[12]

That is not, however, how Luther's view of biblical unity is presented. Typically, the following statement is cited as a summary of Luther's hermeneutic: "All the genuine sacred books agree in this, that all of them preach and inculcate [*treiben*] Christ. And that is the true test by which to judge all books, when we see whether or not they inculcate Christ."[13] Those words give the impression that Christ had to be found in every biblical book in order for Luther to accept it. A notorious example is the epistle of James, which he once called an "epistle of straw" and ranked below the Pauline epistles, 1 Peter, and the Gospel of John.[14] In his 1522 New Testament the table of contents listed not only James but also Hebrews, Jude, and Revelation in a separate group after the other books.

Today it may seem that Luther was playing fast and loose with the sacred text, but it was not the form of the Bible as a fixed canon that mattered most to him but the central message of Christian scripture and the way it was received. That message was called by him the gospel, the good news of salvation history culminating in Jesus the Christ. People in both testaments were given faith and hope, and believers since then still had their faith and hope confirmed and nurtured mainly by scripture. If the Bible or any part of it did not perform that function, then its main purpose was not being served. Both the letter and the spirit of scripture were important, but treating all the words of scripture as equally useful to Christians undermined the priority of the gospel. Once in a while, Luther would cite verses as proof texts, like 1 Peter 3:7 that he invoked against the ordination of women. Most of the time, however, he abided by his own rule: "It is ultimately true that the gospel itself is our guide and instructor in the scriptures."[15]

Authority

The Bible possessed authority because it contained the gospel and disclosed the divine intention for human life. The word of God might have been "sharper than any two-edged sword" (Hebrews 4:12), but it was not to be wielded arrogantly. The authority of scripture required humility before the text. Luther's alleged last words illustrated that humility: "No one can presume to have tasted holy scripture sufficiently unless that person has ruled over the church with the prophets for a thousand years; . . . we are beggars, that is true."[16] Similarly, in the preface to volume one of his collected German works, Luther insisted that theologians begin their study of the biblical text with prayer for illumination and meditative concentration on the passage.

Scripture was, of course, the primary authority to which he appealed in controversy, but the word to be emphasized is *primary*. Luther also acknowledged other authorities, like the writings of early church theologians, but when a doctrine was in dispute, then scripture alone (*sola scriptura*) was the final authority, not the opinion of Augustine or Cyprian or a paragraph from church law. Such was the case at the Diet of Worms in 1521 when Luther uttered the famous words: "I am bound by the scriptures I have quoted and my conscience is captive to the word of God."[17]

That principle did not, however, solve a dispute in which Luther and his opponents appealed to the same passage of scripture but interpreted it differently. At the Leipzig Debate in 1519, he and John Eck both recognized the authority of Jesus's charge to Simon Peter to "feed my sheep" (John 21:15-17), but Eck said it referred to the pope's authority while Luther claimed it meant feeding people with the word of God. Luther was well aware of the danger of subjective interpretation. Scripture was not a wax nose, he said, that can be bent any way the reader desires.[18] Nonetheless, since all believers were priests, all superiors in the church were "to be heard in such a way that everyone of the lowest degree may be free to judge the thought of the superior in matters of faith." Where things of the spirit and faith were involved, it was "absolutely the concern of everyone to see that the priest [the ordained pastor] did not err."[19]

At the same time, Luther recognized a check on individual interpretation of the Bible by allowing the church an important function: "This one thing the church can do: it can distinguish the word of God from human words," even though the church was not above the gospel and could not prove a certain doctrine was true. Under the enlightenment of the Spirit, however, the "mind" of the church could judge and approve doctrines that it recognized were true. "For as among philosophers no one judges the general concepts, but all are judged by them, so it is among us with the mind of the Spirit, who 'judges all things and is judged by no one' [1 Corinthians 2:15]."[20]

For interpreting scripture and ascertaining its authority Luther advocated checks and balances: believers could argue with their pastor's teaching but both pastors and people needed to consider the mind of the church. Both were to be guided by the Spirit and the priority of the gospel and to guard against forcing scripture to support their own opinions. This system did not work very well in the sixteenth century and it has not prevented most Protestants from using the Bible to support their personal views. Nevertheless, Luther's hermeneutic recognizes that the Bible is a book of the church, not the property of individuals, and that all believers have access to the living word of God because the church, under the Spirit's guidance, preserved "a proper grasp of the gospel, that is, the extravagant goodness of God, which no prophet, or apostle, or angel could ever fully express and no heart sufficiently appreciate and absorb."[21]

THEME OF A LIFETIME

In 1531 Luther told the students listening to his lectures on Galatians: "If we lose the doctrine of justification, we lose simply everything."[1] Why such a pronouncement and why did he return to this theme again and again? Because, in the first place, living with the Bible as he did, Luther could scarcely avoid the language of justice and justification. It was present in Psalms, in the prophets, in the Gospels, and in his favorite apostolic writer—Paul: "For we hold that a person is justified by faith apart from works prescribed by the law" (Romans 3:28).

In the second place, justification by faith became the heart of his Reformation agenda. He wanted to teach the freedom of faith that he had come to realize and enjoy for himself. To be free meant to replace works with faith and meritorious religious performance with simple trust in God's mercy. Justification by faith was for Luther a counterproposal to the justification by works that he detected underneath the religiosity of his contemporaries, lay and clergy alike.

In the third place, justification placed Christ again at the center of faith and life. Justification by faith became code language for salvation through the work of Christ alone, not through other mediators like the saints to which people prayed. Luther thought Christ, his "immediate bishop," had practically disappeared from the Christianity of his day, and in *Freedom of a Christian* he subjected it to a scorching critique:

> Who then can comprehend the riches and glory of the Christian life? It can do all things and has all things and lacks nothing. It is lord over sin, death, and hell, and yet at the same time it serves, ministers to, and

benefits everyone. But alas in our day this life is unknown throughout the world; it is neither preached about nor sought after; we are altogether ignorant of our own name and do not know why we are Christian or bear the name of Christians. Surely we are named after Christ, not because he is absent from us, but because we believe in him and are Christs one to another and do to our neighbors as Christ does to us. But in our day we are taught by human doctrines to seek nothing but merits, rewards, and the things that are ours; of Christ we have made a taskmaster far harsher than Moses.[2]

Justification became the theme of a lifetime because Luther's goal, if ever successful, would take longer than a lifetime. He sought to reawaken believers to the presence of Christ in their midst and to the saving power of his work.

This campaign began during his early lectures before Martin became a public figure. The target was scholastic theology and its theory of how people were made righteous or acceptable in God's sight. Nearly two months before the ninety-five theses, Luther prepared a set of ninety-seven Latin propositions to be debated on September 4, 1517. The theses were a broadside against arguments for the human ability to merit salvation. Nominalist theologians had argued that even people in a state of sin could merit the righteousness of Christ by exercising their natural powers to obey the divine commandments. Even though the weakness caused by sin prevented them from meeting the demands of God, sinners could earn the grace that enabled their wills to accomplish perfect obedience and to merit eternal life. There were two kinds of merit, they argued, an imperfect meriting of grace (the righteousness of Christ) with one's natural powers, and then with the help of grace a perfect meriting of eternal life (the righteousness of God).

Between 1517 and 1521 Luther vigorously rejected that merit theology while he worked at redefining both sin and grace. These definitions were presented in his Latin rejoinder to James Latomus, professor at the University of Louvain. Like the medieval schoolmen, Latomus argued that sin after baptism was a weakness that did not prevent the will, assisted by grace, from meriting salvation. At the Heidelberg debate (1518) Luther had argued that sin remaining after baptism was truly sin—a force that prevented the will from meriting salvation. This assertion was also one proposition for which he was excommunicated,[3] but he still defended it later in the same year against Latomus: "In accordance with scripture, we should speak fully of sin . . . as a universal corruption of nature in all its parts: an evil which inclines us to evil from our youth up."[4] With this degree of sin it was impossible for the human will to merit God's righteousness at any point.

Grace, therefore, had to be more than a quality of the soul that made it easier for the will to obey the commandments. Luther rejected that scholastic definition and proposed in its place that grace was an active quality of God, divine favor or mercy, which did not demand righteousness but bestowed it with the gift of faith. Grace forgave the sin and faith began to remove it by purging the sin to which it was opposed.[5] Those who were baptized were not therefore "in sin," argued Luther, even though their sin was not completely removed—because their sin was completely forgiven: "Everything is forgiven through grace, but as yet not everything is healed through the gift."[6] Or in Luther's Latin shorthand: the baptized Christian is *simul iustus et peccator*, at the same time righteous and sinner.

In the Galatians lectures of 1531 Luther tied justification by faith to the person and work of Christ. He endorsed Paul's argument that Christians were no longer under the law because "Christ redeemed us from the curse of the law by becoming a curse for us" (Galatians 3:13). If we attempted to be justified by keeping the law, then we would remain under its curse; but since Christ became a curse *for us*, we are justified by faith in him and are liberated from seeking righteousness through the law.[7] What was this faith, however, and how did faith by itself transfer the benefits of Christ's death to believers? Scholastic theology had argued that faith alone could not do it; faith had to be "formed" or perfected by love in order for the believer to be justified.

Luther responded to this argument in two ways. First, he pointed out the consequences of insisting that faith required love in order to be effective. If love were the indispensable form of faith, believers would have to admit that love was the most important part of the Christian religion. But then, said Luther, "I lose Christ, his blood, his wounds, and all his blessings; and I cling to love and I end up with a moral kind of doing, just as the pope, a pagan philosopher, and the Turk do."[8] In other words, the Christian religion would become a brand of morality that would be hard to distinguish from other ethical systems.

Second, Luther proposed an alternate explanation of how faith operated:

> Therefore Christian faith is not an idle quality or an empty husk in the heart, which may exist in a state of mortal sin until love comes along to make it alive. But if it is true faith, it is a sure trust and firm acceptance

in the heart. It takes hold of Christ in such a way that Christ is the object of faith, or rather not the object but, so to speak, the one who is present in faith itself.[9]

To elaborate the presence of Christ in faith, Luther employed the language of medieval mysticism. It was beyond our thought because there was "darkness," but Christ was present in that "very cloud and faith." How it happened was not the point, but it was not by adding love to faith. In contrast to scholastic theology, "we say it is Christ who forms and trains faith or who is the form of faith. Therefore the Christ who is grasped by faith and who lives in the heart is true Christian righteousness, on account of which God counts us righteous and grants us eternal life."[10]

More attention is now being paid to the influence of mysticism on Luther,[11] and recent Finnish theologians have argued that union with Christ in faith as described in the Galatians lectures was the primary way Luther viewed justification.[12] A different explanation, shared by Melanchthon and other theologians, was the forensic model that Luther also used in the Galatians lectures—almost in the same breath with the mystical model: "Christians are not those who have no sin or feel no sin; they are those to whom, because of their faith in Christ, God does not impute their sin."[13] At stake is the degree to which justified Christians are changed by faith. If Christ is present in their hearts, presumably they have become more like Christ than if God simply overlooked their sin because of their faith. Luther implied many times that justified sinners were more righteous than sinful, but he still used both models to illustrate a process that remained even for him a mystery. In a thesis prepared for debate in 1536 he wrote: "Justification [of the sinner] is a mystery of God, who exalts his saints, because it is not only impossible for the godless to comprehend, but marvelous and hard for the godly themselves to believe."[14]

Luther had to burrow more deeply into how faith worked after he was challenged by another opponent on the subject of the will's power. When the humanist Erasmus was finally persuaded to write against Luther, he chose his theme, as had Latomus, from the propositions for which Luther had been excommunicated: "Since the fall of Adam, or after actual sin, free will exists only in name and when it does what it can it commits sin."[15] Luther had called this assertion a "chief article of the faith," but Erasmus used the free will as a case of how scripture could be cited on both sides of a question.

Before arguing that scripture took an unambiguous stand on the issue, Luther clarified what he meant by saying that free will, in a state of sin, existed in name only. The human will certainly existed as a natural force, but the question was whether or not it had the power to choose, that is, freedom to direct its force toward good or evil when it was under the influence of sin. To have true freedom of choice, the will had to be in a state of neutrality, but for Luther the human will was never in a state of neutrality when it came to matters affecting salvation. It was placed between God and Satan like a beast of burden: "If God rides it, it wills and goes where God wills, . . . If Satan rides it, it wills and goes where Satan wills; nor can it choose to run to either of the two riders or to seek him out, but the riders themselves contend for possession and control of it."[16]

When the Holy Spirit brought the gift of faith to the heart, however, the will was liberated from the power of Satan and sin—not liberated in the sense that the will could now choose freely between good and evil, but freed from the power of sin and directed toward God by the Spirit itself, which made unbelieving wills into believing wills. The Spirit had to hold the will's force in faith, however, because otherwise the sin that remained after conversion would pull the will back under its power:

> If God works in us, the will is changed, and being gently breathed upon by the Spirit of God, it again wills and acts . . . of its own accord, not from compulsion, so that it cannot be turned away by any opposition, nor be overcome or compelled even by the gates of hell, but it goes on willing and delighting in and loving the good, just as before it willed and delighted in and loved evil.[17]

Luther adopted this position because he thought it was Pauline. Romans 1–3 placed all people under sin, and thus the human will, created good, became "ungodly, wicked, and deserving of the wrath of God."[18] Like Paul, Luther viewed sin as a curse that had power to condemn, and salvation was liberation from that curse and its power through faith in Christ. Since faith was a gift, however, it had to be granted by a power that was greater than sin itself, and that power was the divine force of the Holy Spirit, which rescued the human will from its subjection to sin and converted it to believing in Christ as the only savior. Luther therefore accepted the notion of conversion, but it was not a free choice of the will but a powerful intervention of the Spirit that redirected the will to trust in Christ.

Luther's claim on Paul has been contested by New Testament scholars and especially by those associated with the "new perspective of Paul." For example, E. P. Sanders has written:

Luther's emphasis on fictional, imputed righteousness, though it has often been shown to be an incorrect interpretation of Paul, has been influential because it corresponds to the sense of sinfulness which . . . is part and parcel of Western concepts of personhood, with their emphasis on individualism and introspection. Luther sought and found relief from guilt. But Luther's problems were not Paul's, and we misunderstand [Paul] if we see him through Luther's eyes.[19]

Luther did not understand the concepts in Romans exactly the way Paul did, but it was not because Luther was unusually introspective or obsessed with individual guilt. Like Paul, Luther was thinking not just about himself but about a church in which some Christians were convinced they had to fulfill the law in order to be saved. Luther's church was not a community of Jews and Gentiles, and he interpreted the law perhaps more broadly than Paul, but both were arguing that faith in Christ alone and not religious and moral performance brought salvation. For Luther as for Paul, imputation was not the only model that described how faith connected believers with Christ. Both spoke about a union with Christ as well. Luther could also describe salvation in cosmic terms, especially in reference to a favorite verse from Colossians (1:13): "[God] has rescued us from the power of darkness and transferred us into the kingdom of his beloved Son."

Luther became a pillar not because he had the same theology as Paul, but because he transposed Paul's categories into terms that spoke effectively to Christians in his day. Both believed that salvation through faith in Christ was available to all and not merely to those who obeyed the law strictly enough to merit that salvation.

LIVING AS CHRISTIANS

Important though it was, justification by faith was only the first stage of Luther's Reformation agenda. Changing the way Christians lived required not only faith but also the spontaneous result and partner of faith: the exercise of love to the neighbor. Faith and love were the twin anchors of the Christian life; faith enjoyed priority, but love was never absent from the liberated life that faith made possible. In 1525, Luther made that point forcefully in a sermon on Ephesians 3:14-21, which was published as *The Strength and Increase of Faith and Love*:

> To believe inwardly with the heart and to demonstrate that faith outwardly with love are in essence one thing, the result of which is acting, not just talking, and living, not just chattering. The word should not remain stuck on the tongue or in the ears but have force and lead to actions and deeds. In the Old Testament Moses talked a lot but no one acted on those words; here the reverse should be true: few words but much doing. Paul desires that the gospel not be preached in vain but accomplish the purpose for which it is proclaimed.[1]

At the end of the sermon, explaining Ephesians 3:19, Luther declared that love surpassed knowledge and that Paul desired believers to grow in faith, so that it became strong and love was set on fire. Then, as the text said, the faithful would be filled with all the fullness of God and become godlike, not by climbing a stairway to heaven but by living their life on earth filled with God.[2]

Early on, however, Luther and his colleagues recognized that it was not enough to urge people to love. They needed both a conceptual framework and concrete guidance for nurturing faith and exercising charity. That framework was supplied by the concepts of two kingdoms and three orders, and initial guidance was offered by the practical treatises that Luther and his colleagues wrote during the 1520s. Contrary to some accounts, Luther did not invent a "doctrine" of two kingdoms.[3] The term "kingdom" was a biblical concept that emerged from Luther's encounter with scripture and is best rendered "realm." The term "orders," which is best understood as spheres of life, came from Luther's disenchantment with monastic orders and was reclaimed for all the faithful as "true Christian orders."

The notions of two realms and three orders had approximations in medieval thought; Luther adapted them for his agenda but they have been tarnished by modern misuse. In the 1930s Paul Althaus (1888–1966) and others used them to disallow resistance to the Nazi dictatorship because, in their opinion, even unjust governments were divine orders of creation and therefore legitimate.[4] Althaus and his colleagues ignored Luther's many rebukes of tyrannical injustice and used a sharp separation between the spiritual and temporal kingdoms to discourage church leaders from interfering in politics.

Contemporary theologian Risto Saarinen (1959–) wishes to rehabilitate the three orders, because rightly understood they encourage active participation in the public sphere.[5] Originally, Luther described them as "estates" or roles in which people could live out their baptism: "People may bind themselves to an estate that is best suited to accomplish the purpose of their baptism."[6] In his 1528 confession of faith, Luther introduced them as "true religious orders," that is, genuinely Christian orders in contrast to monastic orders and inauthentic forms of the old piety. True Christian orders were ministry, household relationships, and public service, and above these three realms Luther placed "the common order of Christian love, in which one serves not only the three orders, but also serves every needy person in general with all kinds of benevolent deeds, such as feeding the hungry, giving drink to the thirsty, forgiving enemies, praying for all people, suffering all kinds of evil on earth. Behold, all these are called good and holy works."[7] Luther's concept of two realms has also been misunderstood and misapplied. Critics have emphasized the distinction between the realms instead of their interconnection and have faulted Luther for an ethic of quietism—not least because he criticized the violence and bloodshed caused by the peasant uprising in 1525. He has been unable to shed the reputation of acting as a "lackey of the princes," even though he held the "princes and lords" responsible for injustices suffered by the peasants: "As temporal rulers you do nothing but cheat and rob the people so that you may lead a life of luxury and extravagance. The poor common people cannot bear it any longer."[8] Luther himself, of course, was a sterling example of civil disobedience, even though he was careful about endorsing it for others. For evangelical theologians to criticize city councils and princes was risky business because the Reformation depended on political support, but they did it nonetheless.

The notion that Christians lived in two realms originated in discussions between Luther and Melanchthon about biblical texts that could be used to guide Christian action in the early days of the Reformation. A specific occasion was provided by Duke George, who resisted the Reformation in his part of Saxony and suppressed the distribution of Luther's German New Testament. What should evangelical believers do? Should they disobey a ruler who opposed the gospel (as Luther understood Acts 5:29 to mean) or should they always be "subject to the authorities" as Paul had admonished (Romans 13:1)?

The attempt to solve this dilemma resulted in the notion of two realms in which Christians lived. The spiritual realm, on the one hand, was home to "all true believers who were in Christ and under Christ," and if the world were full of "real Christians," that is, true believers, there would be no need for government and its laws.[9] The worldly or temporal realm, on the other hand, was home to "all who are not Christians" and needed the rule of law, that is, those who might be baptized but did not lead a Christian life.[10] "Real Christians" were so outnumbered by nominal Christians that it would be impossible to rule the world without civil government and its law. In the spiritual realm, however, true Christians had no need of civil authority for themselves but used and obeyed it for the sake of their neighbors, whom they lived to serve and on whose behalf

> they may and should seek vengeance, justice, protection, and help and do as much as possible to achieve it. Likewise the governing authority should, on its own initiative or through the instigation of others, help and protect them too, without any complaint, application, or instigation on its own part. If it fails to do this, [Christians] should permit themselves to be despoiled and slandered; they should not resist evil, as the words of Christ say.[11]

In Luther's vision, therefore, citizenship in the spiritual realm impelled earnest Christians to work for justice and the rights of others in the civil or temporal realm, demonstrating that their faith and love were "in essence one thing," as Luther put it. Generally, they did this by obeying the law but, on behalf of others, Acts 5:29 might force Christians to obey God rather than human authority, even though they were willing to suffer mistreatment done to themselves.

Luther's aim was Christian service of the neighbor—not withdrawal from the world or passivity in the face of evil. For and among themselves, Christians would try to live by the Sermon on the Mount, but in the temporal realm Christians found their place in the three orders or spheres of life and put faith to work on behalf of others. The line that separated the two realms was a dotted one that permitted earnest believers to maintain their home in the spiritual realm and still work for the welfare of others in the temporal realm. The line was not a fence that separated Christians from the world.

Some ethical positions taken by Luther did not rely explicitly on the model of two realms, but the reasoning was similar. Faced in 1526 with the Turkish victory over Christian forces in Hungary and the threat of their advance, Luther had to decide if there was ever a case when Christians could use the sword. His answer: Christians could be soldiers and fight in defensive battles to protect their homes, families, and neighbors, but they could not launch a crusade or engage in war for selfish or material gain. If they decided to heed the emperor's call for troops to fight the Turks, Christians would not be on a crusade but helping civil government protect the rights and the safety of everyone in the society.

In *Trade and Usury*, published in 1524, Luther wrestled with ethical conduct in the business world. He was blunt about the obligations placed on true Christians to conduct business according to the Sermon on the Mount. They should not charge interest because scripture said they should lend without expecting anything in return. It was true that Christians could not avoid the world and its practices, but, admonished Luther, in dealing with temporal goods,

> [Christians] should keep in mind these commandments: "What you wish others to do to you, do so to them" (Luke 6:31; Matthew 7:12), and "Love your neighbor as yourself" (Leviticus 19:18; Matthew 22:39). They should consider in addition what they would like for themselves if they were in their neighbors' place. . . . Because we fail to keep our eyes on these commandments and look only at the business deal and its profit and loss, we are bound to have innumerable books, laws, courts, lawsuits, blood, and all sorts of misery. From violation of God's commandments must follow the destruction of God's kingdom, which is peace and unity, in brotherly love and faith.[12]

Luther affirmed that God's creation was good and believed that the temporal realm belonged to God, but he was also realistic about the corruptive power of sin and its social and economic consequences. It was not enough, therefore, for Christians to conduct business as usual; in this sphere they should apply the Sermon on the Mount and let it guide their decisions as they worked for the justice and well-being of their neighbors.

Luther's ethics have been mostly ignored or treated separately from his theology, but his writings about how to live as Christians belonged to theology as snugly as love belonged to faith. "The fact of the matter is," he wrote in 1520, "that I want very much to teach the real good works that spring from faith."[13] Some examples:

From *A Sincere Admonition to All Christians to Guard against Insurrection and Rebellion* (1522): "Urge people not to enter the priesthood, the monastery, or the convent, and hinder them from so doing; encourage those who have already entered to leave; give no more money for bulls, candles, bells, tablets, and churches; tell them that a Christian life consists of faith and love."[14]

From *The Estate of Marriage* (1522): "In the third part, in order that we may say something about the estate of marriage which will be conducive toward the soul's salvation, we shall now consider how to live a Christian and godly life in that estate."[15]

From *Ordinance of A Common Chest* (1523):

> The property of those monasteries that are taken over by the governing authorities should be used in the following three ways. First, those men and women who choose to remain should be supported, as has been said. Second, those who leave should be provided with sufficient funds to find a position and make a fresh start in life, even though they brought nothing with them when they entered the monastery. . . . The third way is the best, however: to devote all the remaining property to the common fund of a common chest, out of which gifts and loans could be made in Christian love to all the needy in the land, be they nobles or commoners. . . . Now there is no greater service of God than Christian love which helps and serves the needy, as Christ himself will judge and testify at the last day (Matthew 25:31–46).[16]

From *To All the City Councils in Germany That They Establish and Maintain Christian Schools* (1524):

> Even though only a single child could thereby be trained to become a real Christian, we ought properly to give a hundred gulden to this cause for

every gulden we would give to fight the Turk, even if he were breathing down our necks. For one real Christian is better and can do more good than all the people on earth. . . . My dear sirs, if we have to spend such large sums every year on guns, roads, bridges, dams, and countless similar items to insure the temporal peace and prosperity of a city, why should not much more be devoted to the poor neglected youth—at least to engage one or two competent teachers for the school?[17]

From *The German Mass* (1526):

The German service needs a plain and simple, fair and square catechism. . . . One must ask what is meant by the first, the second, the third, and the other commandments. One may take these questions from our *Little Prayer Book* [1522] . . . or make others until the heart may grasp the whole sum of Christian truth under two headings or, as it were, in two pouches, namely faith and love.[18]

From *Instruction of the Visitors for Parish Pastors in Electoral Saxony* (1528):

It were well, too, if we did not entirely do away with the penalty of the ban in the true Christian sense described in Matthew (18:15–20). It consists in not admitting to the Lord's table those who, unwilling to mend their ways, live in open sins, such as adultery, habitual drunkenness, and the like. However, before taking such action, they are to be warned several times to mend their ways. Then, if they refuse, the ban may be proclaimed.[19]

From *Against the Antinomians* (1537):

It is surprising to me that anyone can claim that I reject the law or the ten commandments, since there is available, in more than one edition, my exposition of the ten commandments, which furthermore are daily preached and practiced in our churches. . . . The commandments are sung in two versions, as well as painted, printed, carved, and recited by the children morning, noon, and night. I know of no manner in which we do not use them, unless it be that we unfortunately do not practice and paint them with our deeds and life as we should. I myself, as old as I am, recite the commandments daily word for word like a child.[20]

Although not widely acknowledged, Luther taught both the right kind of good works and sanctification; both were actualized through faith and love in the two realms. He warned against identifying holiness with salvation, but even as he gave this warning, Luther affirmed holiness as a characteristic of Christian living in the three spheres of household, government, and church: "To be holy and to be saved are two entirely different things. We are saved through Christ alone, but we become holy both through faith and through these divine foundations or orders."[21] Without his attention to personal holiness and public ethics, which were anchored in faith and not merely a moral code, it would be difficult to claim that Luther was a pillar of theology. With this emphasis, however, his theology becomes credible and relevant to life in every age.

CHAPTER EIGHT

THEOLOGY FOR THE CHURCH

W hen Martin Luther's theology is abstracted from his life and work, it is easy to overlook the purpose of theology for him: it was studied and taught for the *church*. The reforming agenda that was so important for the development of his theology was an agenda for the church, not for theology as a discipline outside the church. The history of Christian thought can be studied as a subject that hardly needs to take church history or church life into account, but for Luther that would have been inconceivable.

At its religious core, the conflict we call the Reformation was a controversy over the following statement from Luther's *Small Catechism* that appears in his explanation of the third article of the Apostles' Creed: "Daily in this Christian church the Holy Spirit abundantly forgives all sins—mine and those of all believers."[1] To explain theologically how forgiveness happened required a redefinition of justification, but to explain how it happened in the actual lives of believers led Luther to redefine both the church and the sacraments.

The meaning of church was revised in stages as his conflict with Rome and the construction of an evangelical Christianity moved ahead. Prior to 1517 he adopted biblical phrases for the church—people of God, faithful congregation, body of Christ—and criticized clergy who failed to preach God's Word. From 1517 to 1521 the conflict over indulgences helped him realize that the church was bigger than Rome and that the Word of God had greater authority than the claims of bishops and popes. As an evangelical church took shape during the 1520s, Luther and his colleagues deliberated what visible forms the church should assume and how its ministry should be defined. After the Lutheran proposal for reunion was rejected by Emperor Charles V in 1530, Luther was forced into a defensive posture that used the Augsburg Confession and Wittenberg theology as a standard for identifying the true church.

That development resulted in the ecclesiology that was summarized in chapter 4: for Luther the church was both a spiritual communion and a public assembly. The spiritual communion of faithful hearts was potentially worldwide and therefore ecumenical; the public assembly materialized at every locale in which believing people gathered to hear the word and receive the sacraments: "Not Rome or this or that place, but baptism, the sacrament, and the gospel are the signs by which the existence of the church in the world can be noticed externally."[2] Those signs or marks of the church's presence were later supplemented by others, but they remained the hallmarks of the true church.

As Luther was listing those signs, he was also reducing the number of sacraments and accentuating the oral transmission of the gospel: "[Christ] called his teaching not scripture but gospel, meaning good news or a proclamation that is spread not by pen but by word of mouth."[3] After completing short pamphlets on penance, baptism, and the Lord's Supper near the end of 1519, he wrote to his friend and the elector's secretary, George Spalatin (1484–1545):

> There is no reason why you or anyone should expect from me a sermon on the other sacraments until I learn by what text I can prove they are sacraments. I consider none of the others a sacrament, for a sacrament can only exist where a divine promise is expressly given and exercises our faith. We can have no communion with God save by the word of him promising and by the faith of the person receiving the promise. At another time you will hear more about their fables of seven sacraments.[4]

Luther never did find satisfactory evidence for declaring confirmation, marriage, ordination, and extreme unction to be sacraments, and in 1520 he withdrew penance from the category of sacraments because he realized that every confession and absolution was an appeal to the promise of forgiveness already bestowed in baptism. Luther therefore replaced penance with baptism as the most important sacrament in Christendom.

That crucial shift was based on two meanings of baptism: Paul's image of dying and rising and God's indelible covenant with the baptized person. The significance of baptism, wrote Luther in 1519, was "a blessed dying unto sin and a resurrection in the grace of God, so that the old person, conceived and born in sin, is there drowned, and a new person, born in grace, comes forth and rises."[5] The dying and rising were so potent that Luther called the life of a Christian from baptism to the grave nothing other than the beginning of a blessed death.[6] Death was blessed because the journey was covered by the "gracious covenant of comfort," according to which the baptized would fight against sin "even to our dying breath, while God will be merciful to us, deal graciously with us and—because we are not sinless in this life—not judge us with severity."[7] Baptized believers should therefore remember their baptism and comfort themselves "joyfully with the fact that God has there pledged to slay sin and not to count it a cause for condemnation."[8] In the medieval church baptism dealt with what had happened in the past, but Luther intended for it to cover past, present, and future with God's promised mercy.

Faith received the promise applied in baptism, and life in the Christian community was dedicated to nurturing that faith. Luther never held that faith was strictly an individual or subjective matter. Faith was personal, to be sure, but in the believing community personal faith was nurtured by external means through which the gospel was proclaimed: preaching, baptism, absolution after confession, the Lord's Supper, and the encouragement and prayer of fellow believers. Luther listed these items in 1537, but he did not call them exactly means of grace but ways in which the gospel "gives guidance and help against sin . . . because God is extravagantly rich in his grace."[9] Grace, or God's favor, was conveyed through external means not as a commodity but as the Holy Spirit granting forgiveness and enabling faith to hold onto God's promise.

Since the Lord's Supper served the same purpose as other means, Luther objected to its traditional meaning as a sacrifice. In this sacrament no offering was made to God except thanksgiving for the divine gift of forgiveness that was declared in the words of institution and received in faith. Luther agreed that the Lord's Supper was uniquely connected to the death of Christ, but as a testament, not as another sacrifice. Jesus, about to die, bequeathed to his followers "an exceedingly rich and everlasting and good testament," for which the sacrament met all the conditions:

> The testator, the oral or written promise, the inheritance, and the heirs
> . . . The testator is Christ, who is about to die. The promise is contained

in the words with which the bread and wine are consecrated. The inheritance which Christ has bequeathed to us in his testament is the forgiveness of sins. The heirs are all the believers in Christ, namely, the holy, elect children of God.[10]

Because it was a testament, the words of institution and the promise of forgiveness they contained took priority over the elements. The material elements—water in baptism and bread and wine in the Lord's Supper—distinguished sacraments from other means and assisted faith by appealing to all the senses. Eating and drinking alone, however, did not convey forgiveness but together with the words "given for you" and "shed for you for the forgiveness of sins." These words, when accompanied by the physical eating and drinking, are the essential thing in the sacrament, and whoever believes these very words has what they declare and state, namely, "forgiveness of sin."[11]

Why then has Luther's view of the Lord's Supper been dominated by the real presence of Christ in the elements? Because it became *the* issue that divided Lutherans from other evangelical or Protestant confessions. His insistence on the real presence was born in controversy with Zwingli and the Swiss reformers. Luther had given up the medieval concept of transubstantiation that explained how the bread and wine became the body and blood of Christ. He did not, however, give up a literal interpretation of the words of institution which, according to his *Small Catechism*, made the sacrament "the true body and blood of our Lord Jesus Christ under the bread and wine, instituted by Christ himself for us Christians to eat and to drink."[12] The preposition "under," sometimes expanded by Luther to "in and under," made his view close enough to transubstantiation for Zwingli to worry that laypeople could not tell the difference.

Zwingli was concerned about the superstition and materialism of medieval piety that he described as worshiping "with embraces and kisses wood, stones, earth, dust, shoes, vestments, rings, hats, swords, and belts."[13] He feared that too much emphasis on the elements would encourage people to continue the superstitious veneration of the elements that he opposed. When he was presented with a more spiritual interpretation of the words of institution, he used it to challenge Luther.

Luther also opposed a superstitious use of the elements, but the words were a clear text that contained the essence of the sacrament, the forgiveness of sins. To interpret "this is my body" as "this bread stands for my body" was to undercut the promise that followed: "given and shed for you for the forgiveness of sins." Referring to the words of institution, he responded to Zwingli:

> On this we take our stand, and we also believe and teach that in the supper we eat and take to ourselves Christ's body truly and physically. But how this takes place or how he is in the bread, we do not know and are not meant to know. God's word we should believe without setting bounds or measure to it. The bread we see with our eyes, but we hear with our ears that Christ's body is present.[14]

The priority that Luther gave to the words over the elements led him to insist on the real presence of Christ in the elements, and, though unintended, that insistence displaced promise and faith from the heart of the sacrament. For some Lutherans it became more important to believe in the real presence than in the promise of forgiveness. Believing in the real presence, however, did not make forgiveness present and effective. Christ was truly present with forgiveness whether recipients believed in the real presence or not. According to Luther, sins were forgiven only when communicants believed the promises contained in the words of institution. Those words strengthened faith and enabled it to embrace the forgiveness offered by Christ with his body and blood.

The controversy with Zwingli was the second occasion Luther had for emphasizing what might be called the objective side of the sacraments and their function as external means of forgiveness. His former colleague, Andrew Karlstadt, more inclined to mysticism than Luther, had already argued for a spiritual function of the Lord's Supper. For Karlstadt the purpose of the sacrament was to connect the mind to the cross of Christ in a particularly forceful way. Forgiveness of sin took place on the cross, not in the sacrament; it should take the recipient back to the cross through spiritual remembrance and faith.

Luther had emphasized faith, but now he feared that faith was being understood so subjectively that the certainty of God's promises was being lost. Suppose the Lord's Supper did not produce the desired inward effect or transport believers to the cross. Even worse, suppose believers began to scrutinize their faith and blame themselves for not believing or being spiritual enough. Then the sacrament would have an effect contrary to its purpose: undermining faith instead of strengthening it and causing believers to doubt their forgiveness instead of increasing their certainty.

For that reason, said Luther, "everything depended on the word,"[15] and believers had to give up trying to return to the cross and let the cross come to them through word and sacrament. "If now I seek the forgiveness of sins," he asserted, "I do not run to the cross for I will not find it given there. Nor must I hold to the suffering of Christ, as Dr. Karlstadt trifles, in knowledge or remembrance, for I will not find it there either. But in the sacrament or the gospel I will find the word which distributes, presents, offers, and gives to me that forgiveness which was won on the cross."[16] He made a similar argument against Zwingli's criticism that he was limiting God by insisting that Christ was present in the sacrament:

> Although God is everywhere, God does not permit himself to be so caught and grasped, . . . because it is one thing if God is present and another if God is present for you! God is there for you when he adds his word and binds himself, saying: "Here you are to find me." Now when you have the word, you can grasp and have God with certainty and say: "Here I have you according to your word."[17]

Luther applied the same "present for you" to all the external means through which the Holy Spirit imparted forgiveness and strengthened faith. God might well be everywhere and God was certainly at work on the cross, but believers were not God. For Luther they were human beings whose minds and hearts were easily distracted and whose confidence was quickly eroded. Luther understood human weakness, perhaps because of his own, and he found the certainty he needed in God's word that was always available in the church. Other believers, too, could be certain that word was waiting "for them" in baptism, absolution, the Lord's supper, preaching, and the encouragement of others.

When infant baptism was challenged by Anabaptists, who insisted that explicit faith needed to precede baptism, Luther fell back on the certainty offered by baptism as a visible, external form of God's word. Faith by itself was unreliable: "For it so happens that often those who claim to believe do not at all believe, and those who do not think they believe, but are in despair, have the greatest faith."[18] But God's promise was always strong and certain, and that promise made the sacrament of baptism valid for people of all ages and levels of faith. Or as Luther put it: "Faith does not exist for baptism, but baptism for faith."[19] He illustrated his argument with personal experience:

> I would compare people who let themselves be rebaptized with people who brood and have scruples because perhaps they did not believe as children. The next day, when the devil comes, their hearts are filled

with scruples and they say: "Ah, now for the first time we feel we have the right faith, yesterday we do not think we truly believed. So we need to be baptized a third time, the second baptism not being of any avail." You think the devil cannot do such things? You had better get to know him better. He can do worse than that, dear friends, he can cast doubt on the third and fourth and so on . . . just as he has done with me and many in the matter of confession. We never seemed able to confess sufficiently certain sins, and incessantly and restlessly we sought one absolution after another, one father confessor after another, just because we sought to rely on our confession, as those to be baptized now want to rely on their own faith.[20]

The importance of knowing with certainty where to find God's word led Luther to support an office of ministry in the church even though he stoutly defended the priesthood of all the baptized. In 1521 he wrote: "I never wanted more than that all Christians should be priests; yet not all should be consecrated by bishops, not all preach, celebrate mass, and exercise the priestly office unless they have been appointed and called to do so."[21] When he defended the right of every Christian assembly to make that appointment, he declared that those who served in the office of preaching had the highest office in Christendom.[22]

After the uprising of 1525 further disrupted parish life, Luther and his colleagues shaped a new evangelical office of ministry. While they composed new orders of worship and wrote catechisms, they also introduced the supervision of pastors and parishes by ministers who were designated superintendents. Because no bishops in Germany joined the evangelical movement, the superintendents took over traditional episcopal functions and their instructions were specific:

The superintendent shall question and examine [pastors] as to their life and teaching and whether or not they will satisfactorily serve the people, so that by God's help we may carefully prevent any ignorant or incompetent people from being accepted and unlearned folk being misled. For time and again and especially in recent years experience has shown how much good or evil may be expected from competent and incompetent preachers.[23]

Gradually, first-time pastors were required to study theology and pass examinations administered by university faculty. At the behest of the elector of Saxony, ordination was reintroduced at Wittenberg in 1535. It was no longer a sacrament, but an induction of pastors into the office of ministry by the laying on of hands—either at Wittenberg or in local parishes the pastors would serve.

Above all, ordaining qualified candidates into the office of ministry certified that they would provide the external means of the gospel to the entire priesthood of believers and assure those believers that the promises of the gospel applied to them. In order to do that, pastors needed theological training and to that end Luther and his colleagues dedicated their own theological efforts. Outside the church and its provision of God's Word, no one could be sure to find a merciful God and forgiveness of sins. In the church, however, by using the means provided by God and offered by the minister, Luther was convinced that everyone could be "kept in the true faith" and daily the Holy Spirit would abundantly forgive all their sins.

CHAPTER NINE

CONFESSING THE FAITH

Luther's faith was unashamedly trinitarian. Presentations that make it seem only personal or utilitarian can appeal to texts like those in chapter 8 that underscore the sacramental "for you" or they can quote a statement like the following from 1519: "Of what help is it to you that God is God if he is not God to you."[1] For Luther, however, the personal power of faith stemmed from its trinitarian foundation. In 1528, fearing that after his death he would be misquoted or his theology twisted, he decided to "confess his faith before God and all the world point by point." He began so:

> First, I believe with my whole heart the sublime article of the majesty of God, that the Father, Son, and Holy Spirit, three distinct persons, are by nature one true and genuine God, the maker of heaven and earth; in complete opposition to the Arians, Macedonians, Sabellians, and similar heretics. All this has been maintained up to this time both in the Roman Church and among Christian churches throughout the whole world.[2]

Luther reported that he had traced the articles of faith through scripture, but he was savvy enough about church history to realize that it took several centuries and many controversies for Christianity to define its most distinguishing feature: the trinitarian nature of God. Identifying ancient heresies here and in his long treatise on *Councils and the Churches* (1539) was one way of keeping the Reformation in the historical mainstream of Christianity.

Luther affirmed the Trinity in other writings of a confessional and cat-echetical nature. His explanations of the Apostles' Creed in the cate-chisms, which are still taught and memorized, are eloquent and concise statements that combine the trinitarian foundation of faith with its per-sonal benefits. Part one of the *Smalcald Articles* (1537), which Luther was asked to prepare for potential negotiations, begins with a strong trinitar-ian statement that he knew the Roman Church also accepted.[3] The state-ments of 1528 and 1537 declared that only the second person of the Trinity became incarnate. Both also elaborated the way in which Luther thought medieval worship and piety had distorted a proper understanding of the person and work of Christ. Luther's affirmations of the Trinity, therefore, had a polemical as well as an ecumenical side.

Luther's statements about God the creator and God the Holy Spirit have received less attention than his thought about God the Son. Hence, to avoid distorting his theology and to appreciate its breadth, his explana-tions of all three credal articles from the *Small Catechism* deserve to be quoted and discussed.

The first of these articles concerns *God the Creator*:

> I believe that God has created me together with all that exists. God has given me and still preserves my body and soul: eyes, ears, and all limbs and senses; reason and all mental faculties. In addition, God daily and abundantly provides shoes and clothing, food and drink, house and farm, spouse and children, fields, livestock, and all property—along with all necessities and nourishment for this body and life. God protects me against all danger and shields and preserves me from all evil. All this he has done out of pure, fatherly, and divine goodness and mercy, without any merit or worthiness of mine at all! For all of this I owe it to God to thank and praise, serve and obey him. This is most certainly true.[4]

Luther did not use the word providence, but that word best describes his appreciation for creation and its creator. He was aware of questions ear-lier theologians had raised about the first chapter of Genesis—for exam-ple, in which season of the year the world was created. His nominalist training, however, made him impatient with speculation about matters that pushed beyond what God had revealed. He was content to reflect "on the divine solicitude and benevolence toward us, because God provided such an attractive dwelling place for future human beings before they were created."[5] In his 1528 confession Luther declared that "the Father gives himself to us, with heaven and earth and all the creatures, in order that they may serve us and benefit us." Although the gift had "become obscured and useless through Adam's fall," the Son "reconciled us to the Father in order that, restored to life and righteousness, we might also know and have the Father and his gifts."[6] With providence, therefore, came both enjoyment and stewardship of God's gifts; and with redemption came not only hope for a world to come but also a fresh appreciation of the present world.

Stewardship is not a theme usually associated with Luther's treatment of the creed's first article, but it may be one of his most useful lessons. More commonly discussed are his emphasis on God hidden and revealed and his designation of creatures as God's masks (*larvae*). Both themes, however, complement the gratitude and responsibility that God's created gifts should inspire in human beings. Luther's caution against speculation was based on the distinction between God hidden and God revealed, or God himself and God's Word. He told Erasmus: "God does many things that he does not disclose to us in his Word; . . . it is our business, however, to pay attention to his Word and to leave God's inscrutable will alone."[7] In his Word God revealed himself as creator and the world as an attractive dwelling place for human beings to enjoy.

Using the term "masks" was another way Luther affirmed that God was providentially active in the world through his creatures. In 1531, as he interpreted Psalm 147, he enumerated the blessings for which creatures ought to thank their creator. The first blessing was protection and security, which was not an achievement of human intelligence or power but a gift of God. God provided those gifts nonetheless through human activity:

> What else is all our work to God—whether in the fields, in the garden, in the city, in the house, in war, in government—but just such child's play, by which he wants to give his gifts in the fields, at home, and everywhere else? These are the masks of God, behind which he wants to remain concealed and do all things.[8]

Even though Luther believed the divine image was severely impaired by original sin, God still worked through human beings. In those who believed the gospel, that image was being restored until "in the kingdom of the Father" the will would be "truly free and good, the mind truly enlightened, and the memory persistent." In the meantime, although impaired, human intellect and will were able to support God's preservation of the earth.[9] Human life cannot be without fear, a result of original sin, but believers can know, taught Luther, whose world it is and whose work is being done when they care for it.

The second article of the creed concerns *God the Redeemer*:

> I believe that Jesus Christ, true God, begotten of the Father in eternity, and also a true human being, born of the Virgin Mary, is my Lord. He has redeemed me, a lost and condemned human being. He has purchased and freed me from all sins, from death, and from the power of the devil, not with gold or silver but with his holy, precious blood and his innocent suffering and death. He has done all this in order that I may belong to him, live under him in his kingdom, and serve him in eternal righteousness, innocence, and blessedness, just as he is risen from the dead and lives and rules eternally. This is most certainly true.[10]

The explanation of the second article shows that for Luther the work of Christ needed to be stressed more than the person of Christ. He never intended to separate them, of course, and in the 1528 confession he offered a fuller statement about the person:

> Second, I believe and know that the scripture teaches us that the second person in the Godhead, the Son, alone became truly human, conceived by the Holy Spirit without human cooperation, and was born of the pure, holy virgin Mary as of a real natural mother, all of which St. Luke clearly describes and the prophets foretold; so that neither the Father nor the Holy Spirit became human, as certain heretics have taught.[11]

These words in part three of *Confession concerning Christ's Supper* were complementary to his discussion of Christ's person in part one. Zwingli had contended that the human nature or body of Christ after the Resurrection was restricted to the right hand of God in heaven and therefore could not be in the bread and wine of the Lord's Supper. Luther responded:

> My grounds, on which I rest in this matter, are as follows: the first is the article of our faith that Jesus Christ is essential, natural, true, complete God and man in one person, undivided and inseparable. The second, that the right hand of God is everywhere. The third, that the Word of God [words of institution] is not false or deceitful. The fourth, that God has and knows various ways to be present in a certain place.[12]

Following the dogma established at Chalcedon, Luther insisted that the two natures of Christ should be distinguished but never separated. After the Resurrection the glorified body of Christ was able to be everywhere (*ubique*) the divine nature of Christ was present; hence the body and blood of Christ, his human nature, were truly present in and under the bread and wine at the Lord's Supper as the words of institution declared. Would Luther have stressed the union of the two natures without the controversy with Zwingli? Perhaps not, but the union of natures—as Luther's explanation of the second article indicates—was crucial to Christ's atoning work as well as to his bodily presence in the supper. Moreover, both the humanity and the divinity of Christ contributed equally to Luther's concept of God:

> And if you could show me the place where God is and not the man, then the person is already divided and I could at once say truthfully, "Here is God who is not the man and has never become man." But no God like that for me! . . . This would leave me a poor sort of Christ, if he were present only at one single place, as a divine and human person, and if at all other places he had to be nothing more than a mere isolated God and a divine person without the humanity. No, wherever you place God for me, you must also place the humanity for me.[13]

Eric Gritsch and Robert Jenson captured the importance of Christ's humanity for Luther's view of God when they titled their chapter on Christology "God deep in the flesh."[14]

Luther explained the work of Christ in a surprisingly flexible manner. On the one hand, he summarized it simply: "The Son himself subsequently gave himself and bestowed all his works, sufferings, wisdom, and righteousness, and reconciled us to the Father, in order that, restored to life and righteousness, we might also know and have the Father and his gifts."[15] On the other hand, he made use of traditional theories of the atonement but without showing a preference for one theory over another. In a sermon on John 14:19, Luther put the "Christus victor" motif in the mouth of Jesus himself:

> Christ defies death, the devil, and the world: "Let them crucify, kill, and even bury me," he says, "yet they will not destroy and devour me. On the contrary, I will drown death in myself and swallow it up in my life, and I will overcome the devil through my power. Now since they cannot keep me in death, even though they attack me with death, I will not leave you in death either. They will indeed kill me physically, but I shall nonetheless continue to live. And if I live, you, too, shall live with me. For I in turn will maul and destroy death in such a way that it will be defeated not only for me but also for you who believe in me. And you will live as long as I do."[16]

Gustaf Aulén argued that Luther preferred the "Christus victor motif,"[17] but in fact Luther readily offered other interpretations of the atonement that sometimes defy categorization. The satisfaction motif is obviously present in an arresting passage from his lecture on Galatians 3:13 ("Christ redeemed us from the curse of the law by becoming a curse for us"): "In short, [Christ] has and bears all human sin in his body—not in the sense that he has committed them but in the sense that he took these sins, committed by us, upon his own body, in order to make satisfaction for them with his own blood."[18] Two chapters later, however, he concentrates on the liberation of the conscience from God's wrath:

> This is the freedom with which Christ has set us free, not from some human slavery or tyrannical authority, but from the eternal wrath of God. Where? In the conscience. . . . For who can express what a great gift it is for someone to be able to declare for certain that God neither is nor ever will be wrathful but will forever be a gracious and merciful Father for the sake of Christ.[19]

Luther was less concerned to explain the atonement than he was to illustrate how the benefits of Christ's work were appropriated by believers. A favorite motif was the "happy exchange" between Christ and sinners, which, in a Christmas Eve postil, he based not on the death of Christ but on his birth:

> See to it that you derive from the gospel not only enjoyment of the [Christmas] story, for that does not last long. Nor should you derive from it only an example, for that does not hold up without faith. But see to it that you make his birth your own and that you make an exchange with him, so that you rid yourself of your birth and receive, instead, his. This happens if you have faith. By this token you sit assuredly in the virgin Mary's lap and are her dear child.[20]

In this case, as in many, the effect of the "happy exchange" and the gospel that contained it were driven home with a practical lesson:

> Nature by itself could not have discovered such teaching [the gospel], nor can the intelligence, reason, and wisdom of anyone devise it. For who would fathom on their own that faith in Christ unites us with Christ and makes us owners of all the possessions of Christ? And who would imagine that no works are good except those which pertain to our neighbor?[21]

Another illustration employed the ancient concept of "becoming god-like" (*theosis*). It occurred in the sermon that was preached on Ephesians 3 and published in 1525.[22] On verse 19 ("And to know the love of Christ that surpasses knowledge, so that you may be filled with all the fullness of God"), Luther offered the following commentary:

> Everything that God is and can do is completely in us and so effective that we are entirely made like God—not in such a way that we have just one part or a few pieces but "all the fullness." Much has been written about the way we are to become godlike. Some have constructed ladders on which we can climb to heaven and others have written similar things, but all that is shoddy work. This passage shows us the truest way to become godlike: be filled to the utmost with God, lacking in no part but having it altogether, until every word, thought, and deed, your whole life in fact, becomes utterly divine.[23]

Like the "happy exchange," his comment on "being filled with the fullness of God" seemed to endorse an unlimited effect of Christ's work on the lives of the redeemed. In this case, however, Luther added the limitation:

> No one should imagine, however, that such fullness can be attained in this life. We may indeed desire it and pray for it, as Paul does here, but we will not find any person alive with that perfect fullness. We must rely alone upon our desire for such perfection and our deep sighing for it. As long as we live in the flesh, we are filled, alas, with all the fullness of Adam. Hence we must pray unceasingly for God to remove our weakness, put courage and spirit into our hearts, and so to fill us with grace and strength that God alone may rule and be fully at work in us. Let us all desire this for one another, and to that end may God grant us grace.[24]

Regardless of how the work of Christ was interpreted, the reality of sin that remained in the Christian life required the effective work of the third person of the Trinity.

Hence, the third article of the creed concerns *God the Sanctifier*:

> I believe that by my own understanding and strength I cannot believe in Jesus Christ my Lord or come to him, but instead the Holy Spirit has called me through the gospel, enlightened me with his gifts, made me holy and kept me in the true faith, just as he calls, gathers, enlightens, and makes holy the whole Christian church on earth and keeps it with Jesus Christ in the one common, true faith. Daily in this Christian church the Holy Spirit abundantly forgives all sins—mine and those of

all believers. On the Last Day the Holy Spirit will raise me and all the dead and will give to me and all believers in Christ eternal life. This is most certainly true.[25]

Apart from the book by Regin Prenter, the place of the Holy Spirit in Luther's theology has been underappreciated.[26] The argument could be made that without the Holy Spirit Luther's words would be true: "Of what help is it to you that God is God if he is not God to you."[27] The Holy Spirit made God a God for us, as Luther's explanation of the third article plainly says. Neither faith in Christ nor the work of Christ would fulfill its purpose if the Holy Spirit did not generate that faith and transmit the benefits of Christ's work to believers. Luther did not neglect the person of the Spirit; his 1528 confession declares that with the Father and the Son the Holy Spirit is "one true God and proceeds eternally from the Father and the Son, yet is a distinct person in the one divine essence and nature."[28] Soon after that statement, however, he proclaims how necessary the work of the Spirit is: "Because this grace [of Christ] would benefit no one if it remained so profoundly hidden and could not come to us, the Holy Spirit comes and gives himself to us also, wholly and completely."[29]

Very little of what Luther says about the first and second articles of the creed would have aroused controversy during the Reformation. Now, however, except for the person of the Holy Spirit in the Godhead, much became controversial as soon as Luther elaborated what the Spirit does and how the Spirit accomplishes it. So what does the Spirit do? "He teaches us to understand this deed of Christ, which has been manifested to us, helps us to receive and preserve it, use it to our advantage and impart it to others, increase and extend it."[30] How does the Spirit do it? "He does this both inwardly and outwardly—inwardly by means of faith and other spiritual gifts, outwardly through the gospel, baptism, sacrament of the altar, through which as through three means or methods he comes to us and inculcates the sufferings of Christ for the benefit of our salvation."[31]

The 1528 confession then demonstrates why those words were controversial. After the general answers just quoted, Luther became specific: he declared baptism and the Lord's Supper to be divine ordinances and spurned those who made the validity of the sacraments depend solely on faith; he defined the church as a universal community of believers under one head, Christ, and rejected the attempts by popes and bishops to confine the church to their jurisdictions; he restricted forgiveness of sin to the church and to the means through which the Spirit worked; he endorsed private confession as long as believers were not required to enumerate all their sins; he dismissed indulgences based on the merits of saints because they undercut the merit of Christ; he allowed prayers on behalf of the dead but rejected praying to saints, private masses, and vigils. He reaffirmed his stand that only baptism and the Lord's Supper were sacraments, called the sacrifice of the mass "the greatest of all abominations," and advised people to avoid or abandon monastic vows.[32] To sum it up, Luther rejected everything which, in his opinion, claimed to transmit the benefits of Christ's death by restricting or distorting the means through which the Spirit brought those benefits. The main benefits of Christ's death, forgiveness of sin and eternal life, were not attributable to human merit but only to faith in Christ that had to be generated and kept alive by the Spirit.

Because the Spirit and not human effort was responsible for faith, Luther also credited the Holy Spirit with rescuing believers from the "monster of uncertainty" that was for him the effect of much late medieval piety. The sighing of the Spirit directed believers away from themselves so that they did not depend on their "own strength, conscience, experience, person, or works," but depended on that which was outside themselves, the "promise and truth of God which cannot deceive."[33]

Finally, Luther granted to the Holy Spirit the role of sanctifier. Sanctification is seldom mentioned in the same breath with Luther's name, but he called it a work of the Spirit in his explanation of the third article, the 1528 confession, and in the *Large Catechism*. In the confession, the distinction he made between being made holy and being saved remained valid for all his comments on Christian holiness. Salvation came through Christ alone, but holiness came through faith, which led to love and service of the neighbor that believers exercised through the genuine Christian orders of ministry, public service, and domestic relationships.[34] In the *Large Catechism* Luther tied holiness more tightly to life in the church. He asked: How did sanctifying take place?

> Answer: Just as the Son obtains dominion by purchasing us through his birth, death, and resurrection, so the Holy Spirit effects our being made holy through the following: the community of saints or Christian church, the forgiveness of sins, the resurrection of the body, and the life everlasting. That is, he first leads us into his holy community, placing us into the church's lap, where he preaches to us and brings us to Christ.[35]

Within the church, however, believers were never without sin and needed full forgiveness every day. As long as daily forgiveness was sought and granted, Luther conceded, grudgingly perhaps, that some progress in holiness could be made:

> Meanwhile, because holiness has begun and is growing daily, we await the time when our flesh will be put to death, will be buried with all its uncleanness, and will come forth gloriously and arise to complete and perfect holiness in a new, eternal life. Now, however, we remain only halfway pure and holy. The Holy Spirit must always work in us through the word, granting us daily forgiveness until we attain to that life where there will be no more forgiveness. In that life there will be only perfectly pure and holy people.[36]

Ultimately, Luther was less concerned about the degree of holiness achieved than about its perdurance and perfection through the work of the Holy Spirit. The third article of the creed, therefore, had to remain always in force:

> For creation is now behind us, and redemption has also taken place, but the Holy Spirit continues his work without ceasing until the Last Day, and for this purpose he has appointed a community on earth, through which he speaks and does all his work. . . . Then when his work has been finished and we abide in it, having died to the world and all misfortune, he will finally make us perfectly and eternally holy. Now we wait in faith for this to be accomplished through the Word.[37]

Luther thought the wait would be short, and he expected the last day and eternal holiness to arrive soon. In 1539, accusing the pope of not making an earnest attempt to reform the church but letting it go to ruin, Luther wrote: "If the last day were not close at hand, it would be no wonder if heaven and earth were to crumble because of such blasphemy. However, since God is able to endure this, that day cannot be far off."[38]

CHAPTER TEN

A KINGDOM OF PROMISE

Martin Luther lived in a Germany that expected the Last Day to dawn at any time. For him, however, that expectation was intensified by the unhappy state of the church. "Is there today," he asked the students in his first lecture course, "anything prouder, more arrogant, more pompous, more boastful than the princes and priests of the church?"[1] He had learned from the Cistercian abbot Bernard of Clairvaux (d. 1153) that no greater danger threatened the church than peace, security, and prosperity. As he prepared for the debate with John Eck in 1519, Luther wondered whether the pope was the antichrist or his apostle, "so miserably is Christ, i.e. truth, corrupted and crucified by the pope in his decretals."[2]

The eschatological tension accelerated as the evangelical movement grew and encountered sharp opposition. In 1530, the year of failed reunion efforts at Augsburg, one year after the siege of Vienna by Ottoman Turks, and four years before the full German Bible appeared, Luther dedicated his translation of the prophet Daniel to the future elector of Saxony, John Frederick, with the following words:

> Grace and peace in Christ our Lord. The world is rushing so diligently to its end that I often fear the last day will break before we can finish turning the holy scripture into German. From scripture we can determine that we have nothing more to expect from this world. All is done and fulfilled: the Roman empire is finished; the Turk has reached his highest point; the pomp of the papacy is disappearing and the world is cracking on all sides almost as if it would break and fall apart entirely.[3]

By 1545, the year before Luther's death, the future of the German Reformation was bleak. Four years earlier theological dialogues between Catholics and Protestants had ended in failure. Hostility between Lutheran and Catholic rulers in north Germany had intensified. Once again the Turks appeared to be a threat. Emperor Charles V was finally weighing a military campaign against the Protestant Smalcald League, one of whose leaders, Philip of Hesse, had lost his political leverage. The Council of Trent, which became crucial to Catholic reform and recovery, was just beginning.

Luther's writings from the period indicated that he was of two minds. On the one hand, anger and disappointment made him more polemical than ever; he vehemently attacked every group he considered to be an enemy of the gospel: Catholics, non-Catholic dissenters, Turks, and Jews. Luther's agenda to bring true Christianity to Germany had not succeeded as he had hoped, and he was especially hard on lax Christians in his own land. In 1541 he wrote: "We Germans have heard the Word of God now for many years, . . . but today it is a horrible sight to see how thankless and ungrateful we have been toward it."[4]

On the other hand, increasing opposition to the gospel was a positive sign, a reason to hope for the approaching kingdom. Early on Luther taught that true Christians were a minority who always encountered hostility and had to bear the cross. Now the antichrist was unleashing a final, desperate assault that looked as if it might succeed. If the world had to stand much longer, he had predicted in 1530, it would become Muslim or skeptical and no Christian would be left. He surmised, however, that the Reformation, which he called "this time of bright gospel light," was being used by God to shorten and restrain tribulation.[5] Three years before his death, Luther expressed satisfaction with what the evangelical movement had accomplished: "I do not leave our churches looking badly; they flourish in pure and sound teaching, and they grow day by day through many excellent and sincere pastors."[6]

In Luther's vision of the future, disappointment and optimism lived side by side, but optimism won out. All along he expected God's kingdom to prevail over the forces of sin that he dubbed the devil's kingdom. Explaining the Lord's Prayer for laypeople in 1519, he had contrasted those two kingdoms. Everyone, he said, can find some trace of the devil's kingdom within, and therefore all must pray for God's kingdom. It begins and grows already during this life "but it will be perfected in yonder life." We are saved, he said, "only when God reigns in us and we are his kingdom."[7]

Luther spoke about the kingdom in us and us in God's kingdom. It worked both ways. Baptism led to the kingdom, as did union with Christ, and both produced a transformation within. Using one of his favorite New Testament verses, Luther said in his lectures on Galatians:

> Christ himself is the life that I now live; in this way Christ and I are one.
> . . . This attachment to him causes me to be liberated from the terror of
> the law and of sin, pulled out of my own skin and transferred into Christ
> and into his kingdom (Colossians 1:13). It is a kingdom of grace, righ-
> teousness, peace, joy, life, salvation, and eternal glory. Since I am in him,
> no evil can harm me.[8]

More than one set of two kingdoms was operative in Luther's theology. The familiar set juxtaposed the spiritual kingdom to the worldly kingdom. Both were ruled by God, one through the gospel and one through the law. The temporal or worldly kingdom, however, was created good and was not identical with the kingdom of the devil, which contained all manner of sin and evil that were opposed to God's rule and would be defeated and re-moved when God's kingdom arrived in its fullness. In the meantime, God's kingdom and the devil's kingdom were fighting over the world, or so Luther portrayed it. He believed the outcome was certain—God's kingdom would win—but for the time being God was checking the devil's might through the gospel in the spiritual kingdom and the law in the temporal kingdom.

That cosmic drama, which Luther deemed biblical, formed the back-drop of his lectures on Genesis delivered over most of his last decade. Luther also called it a conflict between the true and false churches, con-cepts that harkened back to earlier theologians. But however he expressed it, the kingdom of God would prevail because it was a "kingdom of prom-ise" and God had to fulfill his promises. Luther paid close attention to the promises in Genesis, especially the last words of the patriarch Jacob in verse 10 of chapter 49: "The scepter shall not depart from Judah, nor the ruler's staff from between his feet, until [Shiloh] comes to him; and the obedience of the peoples is his." For Luther, Shiloh was Christ[9] and Jacob was referring to promises concerning Christ and his kingdom:

> Jacob depicts a wonderful kingdom, one that is different from the king-
> doms of the world, which are administered through laws and weapons.
> But this is a kingdom of promise. Here God alone is present and works
> all things through the Word. For this is what all the promises and
> prophets teach.[10]

As Luther pondered the next verses, however, he decided they described not only a kingdom of promise but a kingdom in which the promise was fulfilled. In verse 12 ("His eyes are darker than wine, and his teeth whiter than milk") Jacob was describing the wealth of Christ's gifts and the wonderful change they produced in the faithful. Formerly, Luther said, we were afraid of the Last Day and tried to avoid death, sufferings, and hardships. Now we long for the coming of Christ and cry out: "Come, Lord, come!" If we are troubled, he continued, we give thanks to God and are bathed, as it were, in the best wine—the fullness, the abundance, the intoxication induced by the divine promise and gifts of the Holy Spirit.[11] Earlier Luther had said it more concisely: "If you do not believe, you have nothing. Through faith and the promise, however, you already possess the kingdom of God. The communion of saints is completely certain and firm for you, not otherwise than if you were already in heaven."[12]

It may seem hard to reconcile possessing the kingdom of God and being in heaven with life on earth as saint and sinner. Interpreters of Luther have typically painted the side of the sinner so darkly that room scarcely remained for the saint. Throughout his life, however, Luther depicted the power of faith in generous terms—like those above—that have often been ignored.[13] To understand how that was possible when he taught that sin after baptism remained potent, it helps to recall his explanation of the Lord's Prayer in the *Large Catechism*. After enumerating the temptations incited by sin, the world, and the devil, he wrote:

> This, then, is what "lead us not into temptation" means: when God gives us power and strength to resist, even though the attack is not removed or ended. For no one can escape temptations and allurements as long as we live in the flesh and have the devil prowling around us. We cannot help but suffer attacks, and even be mired in them, but we pray here that we may not fall into them or be drowned by them.[14]

For Luther the normal state of existence was not a condition to which he expected to return after a great tragedy was past. If sin, death, and the devil were taken seriously, it was normal for Christians and non-Christians alike always to be under attack. For that matter, the world did not normally enjoy peace, justice, and life that were occasionally interrupted by war, oppression, and death. The opposite was true: war, injustice, and death were everywhere, even when people tried to ignore them, and they were occasionally interrupted by peace and justice. Two things, he taught, made Christian life different: the promises of God and faith in Christ. Together they enabled believers to see more hope than others might have, as if they possessed knowledge and vision that was possible only by surveying history from heaven itself.

In the story of Abraham and Isaac (Genesis 22), the angel of the Lord called to Abraham from heaven just as Abraham put forth his hand to slay his son. Luther assessed that moment as one of several biblical clues to the extraordinary perception of faith:

> This is Christian teaching and wisdom of God, the science of the saints, the sublime knowledge beyond the comprehension of the world: "Death where is your sting? Where is your victory?" (1 Corinthians 15:55). In the midst of death we are in life. "I shall not die . . ." (Psalm 118:17). Let those who have this skill give thanks to God. But we must take pains that we not only speak of it theoretically, but cling to it in fact and with our whole heart.[15]

Luther's kingdom of promise was not so much a doctrine as a reason for believers to hold onto life and hope when the world gave them no reason to do so. Since they realized everyone constantly faced death, relentless temptation, ceaseless conflict, and bitter unfairness, believers could only be comforted and encouraged by faith in Christ and not by their own meritorious efforts. In the midst of a fragile and death-filled world, they clung to the only thing that was ultimately reliable—God's promises—while they remained optimistic and pursued peace, love, and justice in the time that was left. At least that is how Luther saw it and the reason he was able to say, despite much evidence to the contrary:

> So great is the power of faith: it makes us live after we have died. Indeed, in the very hour in which we begin to believe and to take hold of the Word we also begin to live in eternal life; for "the Word of the Lord remains forever" (1 Peter 1:25), and God, who speaks with us, is eternal and will be with us forever.[16]

CHAPTER ELEVEN

BECOMING A PILLAR

In 2017 the Reformation will be five hundred years old. The quincentennial will be marked in many locations but the main celebration will take place in Wittenberg, the town in which it began. In Germany, where Martin Luther ranks among the most-admired historical figures, preparations began in 2007, and the quincentennial will almost certainly surpass the five-hundredth birthday of Luther, which was celebrated in 1983. That occasion was dampened by the fact that Saxony and most of the historical Luther sites lay behind the Iron Curtain. In 2017 a reunited Germany and ten years of preparation should make access and participation much easier.

Most people who recognize Luther's name and make pilgrimages to "Luther land" do not consider him a pillar of theology. They may know that he initiated the Protestant Reformation and suppose that he was a "rebel, genius, [or] liberator," the tagline of Erich Till's 2003 film. Members of Lutheran churches are likely acquainted with his *Small Catechism* and the concept of justification by faith, but most of them know little about his theology or its impact. That awareness is limited mainly to clergy and academics, and that begs the question: why then is Luther regarded as a pillar of theology, at least in western Christianity, especially since he wanted people to study the Bible instead of his own writings?

The answer lies in the two institutions that Luther served, the church and the university, and one that served him, the printing press. Owing to the press, Luther had a head start on every reformer, even Ulrich Zwingli, who did not begin preaching in Zurich until 1519 and whose first Reformation sermon was published in 1522. By that time, Luther was becoming the most published author of religious pamphlets and books in the six-teenth century. According to the founder of craigslist, Martin Luther was a "very good blogger" and became influential through "an early version of the internet."[1] A blogger is not far from an "occasional writer," as Luther was described earlier in this book. Luther wrote pamphlets or preached sermons for many occasions, and his table talk and letters provided a run-ning commentary on highlights of the week. The dissemination of his opinions was more restricted than the reach of modern bloggers, but the new technology broadcast his thoughts to a clerical and academic audi-ence that engaged his ideas and began to build on them.

Luther's writings did not contain a systematic ordering of concepts or a cleanly sequential process of salvation. Before he died students and col-leagues were already disagreeing about what he meant by the bound will, preaching the law, and union with Christ. The conflicts, however, indi-cated that Luther's thought was becoming a norm for evangelical churches that had accepted the Augsburg Confession in 1530 and were starting to call themselves Lutheran. After his death, Lutherans fought over the cor-rect interpretation of Luther's theology in a series of controversies that were only partly resolved in 1577 by the *Formula of Concord*. During the period called orthodoxy, which lasted into the eighteenth century, Lutheran theologians clarified the lines between Lutherans and other con-fessions by insisting that Luther's thought was the proper reading of God's Word in scripture. The manifesto of German pietism, P. J. Spener's *Pia Desideria* (1675), cited Luther more than any other author and argued— only halfway with Luther's blessing—that theology was a practical disci-pline which should "be carried on not by the strife of disputations but rather by the practice of piety."[2] Methodists recall that John Wesley was lis-tening to Luther's preface to Romans when he felt "his heart strangely warmed" and received assurance that Christ had taken away his sins.[3]

In eighteenth- and nineteenth-century Europe, theologians and philoso-phers painted Luther in colors of the intellectual and political currents that influenced them. His writings on freedom and his stand at Worms in-spired German Enlightenment thinkers to create a heroic picture of the re-former as a champion of individual freedom against religious dogmatism—a view of Luther that persists among some Protestants. By contrast, Arthur Schopenhauer (1788–1860) found in Luther support for the power of the human will that the philosopher deemed the primal force of life. Søren Kierkegaard (1813–55) was of two minds about Luther. On the one hand, the priority given to faith was regarded by Kierkegaard as confirmation of his view that truth was subjectivity; but, on the other, he held the misperception of Luther's thought partly responsible for the worldliness of the Danish church. Ernst Troeltsch (1865–1923) portrayed Luther as a medieval thinker with an inadequate ethic for modern social problems because Luther limited love for the neighbor to the private sphere. In the twentieth century this reading of Luther's theology gained currency in some circles owing to the misapplication of two kingdoms and three orders mentioned earlier.

Nonetheless, it was twentieth-century scholarship that made Luther a pillar. The catalyst was the rediscovery and publication of Luther's earliest lectures. Using these sources, Karl Holl (1866–1926), professor in Berlin, delivered on the four-hundredth anniversary of the Reformation an address entitled "What Did Luther Understand by Religion?"[4] This address and other essays by Holl boosted a Luther renaissance that influenced Protestant and Catholic scholars, mostly systematic theologians, throughout the century. Holl focused attention on justification by faith, its effect on the conscience, and Luther's so-called tower experience or "Reformation discovery." As a consequence, these issues dominated Luther scholarship for most of the century, especially in Europe and North America.

According to Heinrich Bornkamm, who traced Luther's influence on German intellectual history, "unlike any other figure, Luther forced [Germans] again and again to ponder the religious, intellectual, and political problems" that beset their lives.[5] The reverse is also true. The issues that confront a specific generation in a particular part of the world also force those who consult Luther's theology to seek new insights from it. This book has argued that Luther's theology was mainly about issues that relate to the third article of the creeds. Many of those issues will remain relevant. How to live as Christians in a troubled world will always challenge the community of faith; so will the nurture of faith, the search for the holy, and the nature of the church. The Holy Spirit will remain an issue as long as Christians disagree over how to identify the Spirit's work. Scarcity, pollution, hunger, and violence make the promise of the kingdom and the care of the earth more urgent. Increasing human control over life and death will cause reconsideration of Luther's insistence that death was the enemy and eternal life to an extent already present in believers.

At the same time, issues related to the first and second articles of the creed appear to be of greater importance than they were in Luther's day. The disappearance of Christendom, the interpenetration of cultures and the proximity of religions to one another, more vocal agnosticism and atheism, the persistence of secularism—all these raise questions about the existence and goodness of God, the uniqueness of Christ, the cause of evil, original sin, the meaning of the cross, and the nature of salvation. Luther said something about all these matters, but what he said in the sixteenth century will by themselves not be sufficient for the twenty-first. His perception of Judaism and Islam was so prejudiced by the anti-Judaism of late medieval Europe, the Turkish threat, and unreliable information that his writings on these topics can be of little help. His harsh rejection of opposing points of view and his insistence on Christ as the only savior are not effective ways to begin dialogue.

His flexible view of the atonement, however, will be helpful, especially his deep feeling for the identification of God in Christ with human suffering and sin. Luther did not construct a coherent theology of the cross, but he did harbor great appreciation for the foolishness of the cross and the divine power it demonstrated because it was power made perfect in weakness. Some liberation theologians have regarded that weakness as passivity. Luther's consistent position was not that victims of injustice should remain passive, but that Christians should hesitate to enter a contest in which the victor is the side that employs the greatest violence. At the same time, he was not a pacifist, and his respect for the power of evil and the structural embeddedness of sin could not be more timely. Religious people who reduce sin to personal immorality or use it to stigmatize the objects of their prejudice will not find much support in Luther's theology. Those, however, who try to curb the effect of self-aggrandizement at the expense of others can appeal to Luther's respect for just laws and government and to his insistence that genuine faith cannot exist without concern for the neighbor.

For Luther the existence of God was not an intellectual issue. God was a divine reality to be respected and to be loved. Was God good? Yes, but not always by human standards of goodness. Otherwise God would not be God. Was God a God of wrath? Yes, but God was not angry at creation but at the sin and evil that corrupted it. Otherwise, evil would not matter, only the strongest would prevail, and the cross would not save. Human reason was a good gift of God, but like other human powers, it could be abused and it was never able to prove that God existed. Faith, hope, and love were gifts of the Spirit that had to be nurtured in the community of faith. Without them Luther could not imagine living in this precarious world.

Living with them, however, was not the same as having religion in the traditional sense. Believing in God, observing rituals, praying, and building temples did not pacify God or make God kinder to one person than another. Thinking that way was idolatry: worshiping the self and its needs above God. Luther's best gift to Christian theology was his reminder that Christian faith was not traditional religion—a way to appease the gods and gain their favor—but a way to know and worship God that placed the world and its needs above one's own desires. For that kind of faith, self-disparagement was not necessary, as indicated by Luther's jocular argument about his own teaching and advice:

> Even if I were a fool and had hit upon a good idea, surely no wise person would think it a disgrace to follow me. And if I were a Turk or a heathen, and my plan were nevertheless seen to benefit not myself but Christians, they ought not in fairness spurn my offer. It has happened before that a fool gave better advice than a whole council of the wise.[6]

Notes

1. Laying the Groundwork

1. For the earliest stages of Luther's fame, see Kolb, *Martin Luther as Prophet, Teacher, Hero.*

2. LW 48:42.

3. On this important point see Hagen, *Luther's Approach to Scripture*; Maxfield, *Luther's Lectures on Genesis.*

4. LW 54:282, no. 3843.

5. LW 44:15–114. The American Edition renders the original German title, *Von den guten Werken*, as "Treatise on Good Works."

6. LW 44:22.

7. LW 40:388.

8. LW 34:287.

9. LW 33 contains the entire work under this title. The Latin, *De servo arbitrio*, is better translated as *Bound Choice.*

10. LW 34:328.

11. LW 51:96.

12. LW 31:343.

13. LW 31:344.

2. Becoming Luther

1. LW 14:45. *Confitemini* is the first word of Psalm 117:1 in the Latin Vulgate version where most of the psalms are numbered differently.

3. Shaping a Theologian

1. WATR 1:146 (no. 352).

2. See chapter 1 above.

3. WATR 3:598 (no. 3767).

4. Eichenberger and Wendland, *Deutsche Bibeln vor Luther*, 7–8; Reinitzer, *Biblia deutsch*, 85.

5. LW 14:284.

6. LW 14:284.

7. Leppin, *Martin Luther*, 85.

8. LW 31:129.

9. LW 31:75.

10. LW 48:12 (April 8, 1516).

4. Two Realizations

1. LW 34:336; WA 54:185.

2. LW 34:336–37; WA 54:185–86.

3. LW 34:337; WA 54:186.

4. Erikson, *Young Man Luther*, 99, 148.

5. WA 8:573; LW 48:331: "In your paternal love you were fearful about my weakness because I was then a youth, . . . and you had learned from numerous examples that this way of life turned out sadly for many."

6. WA 8:573; LW 48:331: "This fear of yours, this care, this indignation against me was for a time implacable."

7. LW 48:335. A cowl is a hood that is part of monastic garb.

8. LW 48:336; WA 8:576.

9. Justus Jonas died in 1555 after serving as a preacher in several locales.

10. LW 48:262 (July 13, 1521).

11. LW 48:262 (July 13, 1521).

12. LW 45:352–53 (1524).

13. WA 12:540.8–15.

14. LW 38:70–71.

15. LW 40:54.

5. Living with the Bible

1. LW 48:225.

2. LW 48:356.

3. LW 48:320.

4. LW 48:320.

5. LW 14:45: "Although the entire Psalter and all of holy scripture are dear to me as my only comfort and source of life, I fell in love with this psalm [118] especially."

6. LW 14:285.

7. LW 14:284.

8. LW 43:108.

9. WA 31/1:153–54.

10. WABr 1:513.1–5 (October 3, 1519).

11. LW 26:4.

12. Hendrix, *Ecclesia in via*, 270–71.

13. LW 35:396.

14. LW 35:362.
15. LW 35:123.
16. WATR 5:317–18 (no. 5677).
17. LW 32:112.
18. LW 14:338.
19. LW 14:341.
20. LW 36:107–8.
21. WA 10/1/1:11.

6. Theme of a Lifetime

1. LW 26:26.
2. LW 31:368.
3. LW 32:19.
4. LW 32:224–25.
5. LW 32:227.
6. LW 32:229.
7. LW 26:277.
8. LW 26:270; WA 40/1:423.15–19.
9. LW 26:129.
10. LW 26:130.
11. For example: Hoffman, *Theology of the Heart*; Leppin, *Martin Luther*, 83–87.
12. Mannermaa, *Christ Present in Faith*, trans. Stjerna; *Union with Christ*, ed. Braaten and Jenson.
13. LW 26:133.
14. LW 34:151.
15. LW 32:92–94.
16. LW 33:65–66.
17. LW 33:65.
18. LW 33:249.
19. E. P. Sanders, *Paul: A Very Short Introduction*, 58.

7. Living as Christians

1. WA 17/1:428–29.
2. WA 17/1:438.
3. Karl Barth may have been the first to call it a doctrine; see Lohse, *Martin Luther's Theology*, 154–55.
4. In 1935 Althaus published *Theologie der Ordnungen*. He had signed the Ansbacher Ratschlag of 1934, an attempt to refute the Barmen Declaration. See Ericksen, "The Political Theology of Paul Althaus," and *Theologians under Hitler*. For a summary, see Lazareth, *Christians in Society*, 7–8.
5. Saarinen, "Ethics in Luther's Theology: The Three Orders."
6. LW 35:41.
7. LW 37:364–65.
8. LW 46:19.

9. LW 45:88–89.
10. LW 45:90–91.
11. LW 45:101.
12. LW 45:293.
13. LW 44:24.
14. LW 45:68.
15. LW 45:35.
16. LW 45:172.
17. LW 45:350.
18. LW 53:64, 66.
19. LW 40:311.
20. LW 47:109.
21. LW 37:365.

8. Theology for the Church

1. *The Book of Concord*, ed. Kolb and Wengert, 356.
2. LW 39:75.
3. LW 35:123.
4. WABr 1:594–95 (December 18, 1519).
5. LW 35:30.
6. LW 35:31.
7. LW 35:33, 35.
8. LW 35:35.
9. *Smalcald Articles* 3:4, in *The Book of Concord*, ed. Kolb and Wengert, 319.
10. LW 36:179–80.
11. *Small Catechism*, in *The Book of Concord*, ed. Kolb and Wengert, 363.
12. *Small Catechism*, in *The Book of Concord*, ed. Kolb and Wengert, 362.
13. CR 90:774–75.
14. LW 37:29.
15. LW 40:214.
16. LW 40:214.
17. LW 37:68.
18. LW 40:241.
19. LW 40:246.
20. LW 40:240.
21. LW 39:233.
22. LW 39:314.
23. LW 40:313–14.

9. Confessing the Faith

1. LW 42:8.
2. LW 37:360, 361.
3. *The Book of Concord*, ed. Kolb and Wengert, 300.
4. *The Book of Concord*, ed. Kolb and Wengert, 354–55.

5. LW 1:39.

6. LW 37:366.

7. LW 33:140.

8. LW 14:114. "Just such child's play" is a reference to children praying and hanging stockings in order to receive presents from the Christ child or St. Nicholas. The point is: whatever we do is simply a vehicle for receiving God's gifts.

9. LW 1:62–65.

10. *The Book of Concord*, ed. Kolb and Wengert, 355.

11. LW 37:361.

12. LW 37:214.

13. LW 37:218–19.

14. Gritsch and Jenson, *Lutheranism*, 91.

15. LW 37:366.

16. LW 24:136.

17. Aulén's *Christus Victor* was first published in 1931. For a critique of Aulén see Althaus, *Theology of Martin Luther*, 218–23.

18. LW 26:277.

19. LW 27:4.

20. LW 52:16.

21. LW 52:18.

22. See chapter 7.

23. WA 17/1:438.

24. WA 17/1:438.

25. *The Book of Concord*, ed. Kolb and Wengert, 355–56.

26. Prenter, *Spiritus Creator*.

27. LW 42:8.

28. LW 37:365–66.

29. LW 37:366.

30. LW 37:366.

31. LW 37:366.

32. LW 37:366–71.

33. LW 26:387.

34. LW 37:364–65.

35. *The Book of Concord*, ed. Kolb and Wengert, 435–36.

36. *The Book of Concord*, ed. Kolb and Wengert, 438.

37. *The Book of Concord*, ed. Kolb and Wengert, 439.

38. LW 41:13.

10. A Kingdom of Promise

1. WA 3:421.

2. LW 48:114 (March 13, 1519).

3. WADB 11/2:381.

4. LW 43:219.

5. WADB 11/2:381.

6. WABr 10:335 (June 20, 1543).

7. LW 42:40–41.

8. LW 26:167.

9. The Hebrew word "shiloh" is translated as "tribute" in the NRSV, but in Luther's day it was considered a prophecy of the Messiah.

10. LW 8:264.

11. LW 8:259–60.

12. LW 8:184.

13. For example, in his preface to the book of Romans: LW 35:370–71.

14. *The Book of Concord*, ed. Kolb and Wengert, 454.

15. LW 4:120.

16. LW 8:190.

11. Becoming a Pillar

1. "Martin Luther Was a Blogger," *Der Spiegel Online* (February 14, 2007).

2. Spener, *Pia Desideria*, trans. Tappert, 50; Wallmann, *Philipp Jacob Spener*, 240–41.

3. *The Journals of John Wesley*, 51.

4. Holl, *Luther*, 1–110; Holl, *What Did Luther Understand by Religion?*

5. Bornkamm, *Luther im Spiegel der deutschen Geistesgeschichte*, 13.

6. LW 45:378.

BIBLIOGRAPHY

Primary Sources

Luther's Works, American Edition (LW). 55 vols. Edited by J. Pelikan and H. Lehmann. St. Louis & Philadelphia: Concordia & Fortress, 1955–86. Available on CD-ROM.

Luther's Works, Weimar Edition (*D. Martin Luthers Werke: Kritische Gesamtausgabe*). Weimar: Böhlau, 1883–. *Schriften* (WA), 81 vols. *Briefe* (WABr), 18 vols. *Deutsche Bibel* (WADB), 12 vols. *Tischreden* (WATR), 6 vols. *Archiv zur Weimarer Ausgabe* (AWA) 8 vols.

Luther's "September Bible" in Facsimile. Historical Introduction by Kenneth A. Strand. Ann Arbor: Ann Arbor Publishers, 1972.

The 1529 Holy Week and Easter Sermons of Dr. Martin Luther. Translated by Irving L. Sandberg; annotated and introduced by Timothy J. Wengert. St. Louis: Concordia, 1999.

Luther on Women: A Sourcebook. Edited by Susan Karant-Nunn and Merry Wiesner-Hanks. Cambridge: Cambridge University Press, 2003.

Luther's Spirituality. Edited and translated by Philip D. W. Krey and Peter D. S. Krey. New York & Mahwah, N.J.: Paulist Press, 2008.

Small Catechism, Large Catechism, Smalcald Articles. Translated by Timothy J. Wengert, James Schaaf, William Russell. In *The Book of Concord: The Confessions of the Evangelical Lutheran Church.* Edited by Robert Kolb and Timothy J. Wengert. Minneapolis: Fortress, 2000.

Wesley, John. *The Journals of John Wesley as Abridged by Nehemiah Curnock.* New York: G. P. Putnam's Sons, 1963.

Zwingli, Ulrich. *Huldreich Zwinglis Sämtliche Werke.* Berlin, Leipzig, Zurich, 1905– (*Corpus Reformatorum* [CR] 88ff.).

Research, Introductions, Impact

Anderson, Mary E. *Gustaf Wingren and the Swedish Luther Renaissance.* New York: Peter Lang, 2006.

Arand, Charles P. *That I May Be His Own: An Overview of Luther's Catechisms.* St. Louis: Concordia Academic Press, 2000.

Bornkamm, Heinrich. *Luther im Spiegel der deutschen Geistesgeschichte.* 2nd ed. Göttingen: Vandenhoeck and Ruprecht, 1970.

The Cambridge Companion to Martin Luther. Edited by Donald K. McKim. Cambridge: Cambridge University Press, 2003.

Ericksen, Robert P. "The Political Theology of Paul Althaus." *German Studies Review* 9:3 (October 1986): 547–67.

———. *Theologians under Hitler.* New Haven: Yale University Press, 1985.

Hendrix, Scott H. "American Luther Research in the Twentieth Century." *Lutheran Quarterly* 15 (2001): 1–23.

———. "Martin Luther, Reformer." In *Cambridge History of Christianity.* Vol. 6: *Reformation and Expansion 1500–1660.* Edited by Ronnie Hsia, 3–19. Cambridge & New York: Cambridge University Press, 2007.

Junghans, Helmar. *Martin Luther und Wittenberg.* Munich & Berlin: Koehler & Amelang, 1996.

Kolb, Robert. *Martin Luther As Prophet, Teacher, and Hero: Images of the Reformer, 1520–1620.* Grand Rapids: Baker, 1999.

Lohse, Bernhard. *Martin Luther: Eine Einführung in sein Leben und sein Werk.* 3rd ed. Munich: C. H. Beck, 1997.

Moeller, Bernd. *Luther-Rezeption.* Edited by Johannes Schilling. Göttingen: Vandenhoeck & Ruprecht, 2001.

Pauck, Wilhelm. *From Luther to Tillich: The Reformers and Their Heirs.* Edited by Marion Pauck. San Francisco: Harper & Row, 1984.

Pelikan, Jaroslav. *Interpreters of Luther.* Philadelphia: Fortress, 1968.

Spener, Philip Jacob. *Pia Desideria.* Translated and edited by Theodore G. Tappert. Philadelphia: Fortress, 1964.

Union with Christ: The New Finnish Interpretation of Luther. Edited by Carl E. Braaten and Robert W. Jenson. Grand Rapids & Cambridge, UK: Eerdmans, 1998.

Wallmann, Johannes. *Philipp Jacob Spener und die Anfänge des Pietismus.* Tübingen: Mohr Siebeck, 1970.

———. "The Reception of Luther's Writings on the Jews from the Reformation to the End of the 19th Century." *Lutheran Quarterly* 1 (1987): 72–97.

Life and Times

Bainton, Roland H. *Here I Stand: A Life of Martin Luther.* New York & Nashville: Abingdon, 1950.

Bornkamm, Heinrich. *Luther in Mid-Career 1521–1530.* Edited by Karin Bornkamm. Translated by E. Theodore Bachmann. Philadelphia: Fortress, 1983.

Brecht, Martin. *Martin Luther.* 3 vols. Translated by James L. Schaaf. Philadelphia and Minneapolis: Fortress, 1985–1993.

Edwards, Mark U., Jr. *Luther and the False Brethren.* Stanford: Stanford University Press, 1975.

———. *Luther's Last Battles: Politics and Polemics 1531–1546.* Ithaca: Cornell University Press, 1983.

Erikson, Erik H. *Young Man Luther: A Study in Psychoanalysis and History.* New York: W. W. Norton, 1958.

Gritsch, Eric W. *Martin—God's Court Jester: Luther in Retrospect*. Philadelphia: Fortress, 1983.

Haile, H. G. *Luther: An Experiment in Biography*. Garden City: Doubleday, 1980.

Hendrix, Scott H. "Beyond Erikson: The Relational Luther." *Gettysburg Seminary Bulletin* 75 (Winter 1995): 3–11.

———. *Luther and the Papacy: Stages in a Reformation Conflict*. Philadelphia: Fortress, 1981.

Junghans, Helmar. "Martin Luther: Exploring His Life and Times, 1483–1546." CD-ROM. Minneapolis: Fortress, 1999.

Kittelson, James M. *Luther the Reformer: The Story of the Man and His Career*. Minneapolis: Augsburg, 1986.

Leppin, Volker. *Martin Luther*. Darmstadt: Wissenschaftliche Buchgesellschaft, 2006.

Luther: Rebel, Genius, Liberator. Feature Film directed by Eric Till. 2003.

Marius, Richard. *Martin Luther: The Christian between God and Death*. Cambridge, MA, & London: Harvard University Press, 1999.

Marty, Martin. *Martin Luther*. New York: Viking/Penguin, 2004.

Oberman, Heiko A. *Luther: Man between God and the Devil*. New Haven & London, 1989.

Smith, Jeanette C. "Katharina von Bora through Five Centuries: A Historiography." *Sixteenth Century Journal* 30 (1999): 745–74.

Spitz, Lewis W. *Luther and German Humanism*. Aldershot, UK, & Brookfield, Vt.: Ashgate, 1996.

Steinmetz, David C. *Luther and Staupitz*. Durham: Duke University Press, 1980.

Treu, Martin. *Katharina von Bora*. Wittenberg: Drei Kastanien Verlag, 1995.

Wengert, Timothy J. "Melanchthon and Luther / Luther and Melanchthon." *Lutherjahrbuch* 66 (1999): 55–88.

Theology

Althaus, Paul. *The Ethics of Martin Luther*. Translated by Robert C. Schultz. Philadelphia: Fortress, 1972.

———. *The Theology of Martin Luther*. Translated by Robert C. Schultz. Philadelphia: Fortress, 1966.

Bayer, Oswald. *Living by Faith: Justification and Sanctification*. Translated by G. W. Bromiley. Grand Rapids & Cambridge, UK: Eerdmans, 2003.

Cranz, F. Edward. *An Essay on the Development of Luther's Thought on Justice, Law, and Society*. 2nd ed. Mifflintown, Pa.: Sigler Press, 1998.

Ebeling, Gerhard. *Luther: An Introduction to His Thought*. Translated by R. A. Wilson. Philadelphia: Fortress, 1970.

Forell, George W. *Faith Active in Love*. Minneapolis: Augsburg, 1964.

Gassmann, Günther, and Scott Hendrix. *Fortress Introduction to the Lutheran Confessions*. Minneapolis: Fortress, 1999.

Gerrish, Brian A. *Grace and Reason*. Oxford: Oxford University Press, 1962.

Gritsch, Eric W., and Robert W. Jenson. *Lutheranism: The Theological Movement and Its Confessional Writings*. Philadelphia: Fortress, 1976.

Helmer, Christine. *The Trinity and Martin Luther*. Mainz: Philipp von Zabern, 1999.

Hendrix, Scott H. *Tradition and Authority in the Reformation*. Aldershot, UK, & Brookfield, Vt.: Ashgate, 1996.

Hoffman, Bengt R. *Theology of the Heart: The Role of Mysticism in the Theology of Martin Luther.* Edited by Pearl W. Hoffman. Minneapolis: Kirk House, 1998.

Holl, Karl. *Luther.* 7th ed. Tübingen: Mohr Siebeck, 1948.

————. *What Did Luther Understand by Religion?* Edited by James Luther Adams and Walter F. Bense. Translated by Fred W. Meuser and Walter R. Wietzke. Philadelphia: Fortress, 1977.

Lazareth, William. *Christians in Society: Luther, the Bible, and Social Ethics.* Minneapolis: Fortress, 2001.

Lohse, Bernhard. *Martin Luther's Theology.* Translated and edited by Roy A. Harrisville. Minneapolis: Fortress, 1999.

Mannermaa, Tuomo. *Christ Present in Faith: Luther's View of Justification.* Translated by Kirsi Stjerna. Minneapolis: Fortress, 2005.

Paulson, Steven. *Luther for Armchair Theologians.* Louisville: Westminster John Knox, 2004.

Russell, William R. *Luther's Theological Testament: The Schmalkald Articles.* Minneapolis: Fortress, 1995.

Steinmetz, David C. *Luther in Context.* Bloomington: Indiana University Press, 1986.

Watson, Philip S. *Let God Be God!* Philadelphia: Muhlenberg, 1947.

Wicks, Jared. *Luther's Reform: Studies on Conversion and the Church.* Mainz: Philipp von Zabern, 1992.

Topical Studies

Althaus, Paul. *Theologie der Ordnungen.* Gütersloh: C. Bertelsmann, 1935.

Aulén, Gustaf. *Christus Victor: An Historical Study of the Three Main Types of the Idea of Atonement.* New York: Macmillan, 1951.

Braaten, Carl. "The Doctrine of Two Kingdoms Re-Examined." *Currents in Theology and Mission* 15 (1988): 497–504.

Chung, Paul. *Luther and Buddhism: Aesthetics of Suffering.* Eugene, Ore.: Wipf & Stock, 2000.

Eichenberger, Walter, and Henning Wendland, *Deutsche Bibeln vor Luther.* Hamburg: Friedrich Wittig Verlag, 1977.

Estes, James M. *Peace, Order, and the Glory of God: Secular Authority and the Church in the Thought of Luther and Melanchthon 1518–1559.* Leiden & Boston: Brill, 2005.

Hagen, Kenneth. *Luther's Approach to Scripture As Seen in His "Commentaries" on Galatians 1519–1538.* Tübingen: Mohr Siebeck, 1993.

Harvesting Martin Luther's Reflections on Theology, Ethics, and the Church. Edited by Timothy Wengert. Grand Rapids: Eerdmans, 2004.

Headley, John M. *Luther's View of Church History.* New Haven: Yale University Press, 1963.

Hendrix, Scott H. "The Kingdom of Promise: Disappointment and Hope in Luther's Later Ecclesiology." *Lutherjahrbuch* 71 (2004) 37–60.

Hillerbrand, Hans J. "Martin Luther and the Jews." In *Jews and Christians: Exploring the Past, Present, and Future.* Edited by James H. Charlesworth, 127–50. New York: Crossroad, 1990.

Kreitzer, Beth. *Reforming Mary: Changing Images of the Virgin Mary in Lutheran Sermons of the Sixteenth Century.* Oxford & New York: Oxford University Press, 2004.

Leaver, Robin A. *Luther's Liturgical Music: Principles and Implications.* Grand Rapids & London: Eerdmans, 2007.

Lienhard, Marc. *Luther: Witness to Jesus Christ.* Minneapolis: Augsburg, 1982.

Maxfield, John A. *Luther's Lectures on Genesis and the Formation of Evangelical Identity.* Kirksville: Truman State University, 2008.

McGrath, Alister. *Luther's Theology of the Cross: Martin Luther's Theological Breakthrough.* Oxford: Blackwell, 1990.

Pelikan, Jaroslav. *Luther the Expositor.* St. Louis: Concordia, 1959.

Prenter, Regin. *Spiritus Creator.* Translated by John M. Jensen. Philadelphia: Muhlenberg Press, 1953.

Reinis, Austra. *Reforming the Art of Dying.* Aldershot, UK, & Burlington, Vt.: Ashgate, 2007.

Reinitzer, Heimo. *Biblia deutsch: Luthers Bibelübersetzung und ihre Tradition.* Wolfenbüttel: Herzog August Bibliothek, 1983.

Saarinen, Risto. "Ethics in Luther's Theology: The Three Orders." *Seminary Ridge Review* 5:2 (2003): 37–53.

Trigg, Jonathan. *Baptism in the Theology of Martin Luther.* Leiden: Brill, 1994.

Vajta, Vilmos. *Luther on Worship.* Philadelphia: Fortress, 1958.

Wisløff, Carl. *The Gift of Communion: Luther's Controversy with Rome on Eucharistic Sacrifice.* Minneapolis: Augsburg, 1964.

INDEX